The People's Bible Teachings

CHRIST

He Is My Lord

Harlyn J. Kuschel

NORTHWESTERN PUBLISHING HOUSE
Milwaukee, Wisconsin

All Scripture quotations, unless otherwise indicated, are taken from the HOLY BIBLE, NEW INTERNATIONAL VERSION®. NIV®. Copyright © 1973, 1978, 1984 by International Bible Society. Used by permission of Zondervan. All rights reserved.

The "NIV" and "New International Version" trademarks are registered in the United States Patent and Trademark Office by International Bible Society. Use of either trademark requires the permission of International Bible Society.

All hymns, unless otherwise indicated, are taken from *Christian Worship: A Lutheran Hymnal.* (CW) © 1993 by Northwestern Publishing House.

All rights reserved. No part of this publication may be reproduced, stored in a retrieval system, or transmitted in any form or by any means—electronic, mechanical, photocopying, recording, or otherwise—except for brief quotations in reviews, without prior permission from the publisher.

Library of Congress Control Number: 2006925589
Northwestern Publishing House
1250 N. 113th St., Milwaukee, WI 53226-3284
www.nph.net
© 2007 by Northwestern Publishing House
Published 2007
Printed in the United States of America
ISBN 978-0-8100-1989-8

Table of Contents

Editor's Preface 5

Introduction 7

Part I: THE PERSON OF CHRIST 11

    1. Jesus Christ Is True God 13

    2. Jesus Christ Is True Man 25

    3. The Virgin Birth 35

    4. The Personal Union 41

    5. The Communion of Properties 51

    6. Applying the Doctrine of the
       Two Natures of Christ 63

Part II: THE HUMILIATION AND EXALTATION
        OF CHRIST 69

    7. The "Beggar's Cloak" 71

    8 Return to Power and Glory 83

Part III: THE THREEFOLD OFFICE OF CHRIST 97

    9. Christ the High Priest 99

    10. High Priest after the Order
        of Melchizedek 113

11. Christ the Prophet	119
12. Christ the King	127
Part IV THE WORK OF CHRIST	137
13. Redemption	139
Endnotes	151
For Further Reading	155
Scripture Index	157
Subject Index	163

Editor's Preface

The People's Bible Teachings is a series of books on all of the main doctrinal teachings of the Bible.

Following the pattern set by The People's Bible series, these books are written especially for laypeople. Theological terms, when used, are explained in everyday language so that people can understand them. The authors show how Christian doctrine is drawn directly from clear passages of Scripture and then how those doctrines apply to people's faith and life. Most importantly, these books show how every teaching of Scripture points to Christ, our only Savior.

The authors of The People's Bible Teachings are parish pastors and professors who have had years of experience teaching the Bible. They are men of scholarship and practical insight.

We take this opportunity to express our gratitude to Professor Leroy Dobberstein of Wisconsin Lutheran Seminary, Mequon, Wisconsin, and Professor Thomas Nass of Martin Luther College, New Ulm, Minnesota, for serving as consultants for this series. Their insights and assistance have been invaluable.

We pray that the Lord will use these volumes to help his people grow in their faith, knowledge, and understanding of his saving teachings, which he has revealed to us in the Bible. To God alone be the glory.

Curtis A. Jahn
Series Editor

Introduction

It was on a teaching retreat in Caesarea Philippi, some 30 miles north of the Sea of Galilee, that Jesus posed a question to his disciples. It was an important question, the most important question he would ever ask them. Their answer to the question would define their relationship to him, not just for the relatively brief time he was with them on earth but for all eternity. Still today, it's the most important question that confronts every human being. The answer that each person gives defines also his or her relationship with Jesus, both for now and for all eternity.

Matthew records this key incident in Jesus' ministry in chapter 16 of his gospel. Jesus began the conversation by asking the leading question, "Who do people say the Son of Man is?" (verse 13). The disciples replied by giving a random sampling of the opinions that various people held about him. Most people, it seemed, regarded Jesus as an extraordinary teacher, perhaps even one of the Old Testament prophets come back to life. Then Jesus asked the disciples directly, "But what about you? . . . Who do you say I am?" (verse 15). To that question Peter, acting as the spokesman for all the disciples, gave a simple and direct, yet clear and powerful answer: "You are the Christ," he said, "the Son of the living God" (verse 16). This confession showed that the disciples were convinced beyond all doubt that Jesus was more than a great prophet, more than an ordinary human being. What they had seen and heard from him had led them to the inescapable conclusion that Jesus was the Christ. He was the promised Messiah of God; he was the eternal second person of the Holy Trinity.

Jesus accepted the disciples' confession. He assured them that their confession and the faith in him from which it flowed made them blessed. Nor were their faith and their confession the result of human insight or critical thinking. They were gifts of God to them. Through Jesus' words and deeds, the heavenly Father had revealed him to them as the Christ. And the Holy Spirit had worked in their hearts the faith that accepted, believed, and confessed that saving truth.

After Pentecost, Peter and the rest of the apostles shared their faith and their confession. They personally witnessed for Christ, as the ascended Lord used them to plant his New Testament church. And, inspired by the Holy Spirit, they penned the sacred writings that have been preserved to us in the New Testament Scriptures. Taking its cue from the witness of the apostles, the early church confessed its faith with the simple statement "Jesus is Lord." All the ancient creeds, confessional writings, and liturgies of the Christian church repeat and reaffirm that great refrain. The confession that "Jesus Christ is Lord" distinguishes the Christian faith from all others.

The question, "Who do you say Jesus is?" continues to be one that demands an answer. It will not go away. In the third millennium, no less than in the first century, human beings are sharply divided in their answers to that question. Some, like Jesus' enemies during his earthly ministry, regard him as a fraud. Some question whether he ever really existed. Some, in more flattering terms, call him a *man of universal destiny* or *the kind of person I know I should be*. They place him in a small, elite class of human beings, along with people like Mohammed, Joan of Arc, Gandhi, Martin Luther King Jr. But even those who claim to honor Jesus as an extraordinary teacher and humanitarian fall short of recognizing him as more than a human being. They do not honor him as the God-man and the world's Savior.

Today, tomorrow, and on into eternity, there is and can be only one correct answer to the question, Who is Jesus? That answer cannot be discovered by human reason, scholarship, or logic. It is still revealed to sinful people only by the Father in heaven. It is made the living confession of believers by the Holy Spirit's work in their hearts through the gospel. Jesus is the Christ, the Son of the living God. On the truth that Jesus is Lord rests all the redemptive value of his work, all his authority as our guide, all our hope for his help, and all his right to our worship and praise. On this truth rests the eternal future of every human being, including each of us. Our answer to the question, Who is Jesus Christ? will determine our approach to all other teachings of Scripture as well. In one way or another, all the scriptural truths set forth in every other volume of this People's Bible Teachings series—including justification, law and gospel, the Trinity, the last things, Baptism, the Lord's Supper, and even Christian freedom and sanctification—will rest on the truths that deal with the person and work of Jesus Christ. Knowing Jesus is, indeed, the key to knowing and understanding the Scriptures.

In this little volume we will take a closer look at the Bible's answer to the question, Who is Jesus Christ? The great truths of the person and work of our Savior are set forth very clearly and very directly in both the Old and New Testament Scriptures. May a study of these truths strengthen each reader in the personal conviction that Jesus Christ is Lord, yes, Jesus Christ is *my* Lord. And may it encourage us to share the good news of that Lord and the world's Savior with others.

Part I

THE PERSON OF CHRIST

1

Jesus Christ Is True God

We believe that Jesus Christ is the eternal Son of God, one with the Father from all eternity (John 1:1,2). In the course of time, he took a true and complete, yet sinless, human nature to himself (Galatians 4:4) when he was conceived as a holy child in the virgin Mary through a miracle of the Holy Spirit (Luke 1:35). . . . Jesus Christ is unique, for in him the true God and a true human nature are inseparably united in one person, the holy God-man. He is called Immanuel, which means "God with us" (Matthew 1:23).[1]

These words from *This We Believe*, a confessional statement of the Wisconsin Evangelical Lutheran Synod, clearly and carefully state what Holy Scripture teaches about the person of Christ. That Jesus is indeed true God and true man in one person is one of the most important truths of the Christian faith. It provides us with the key to understanding everything else the Bible teaches about Jesus and his work of bringing about mankind's salvation.

Because it is also a teaching that has been frequently challenged from both outside and inside the Christian church, the doctrine of the two natures of Christ has, down through the ages, been carefully studied and defined by the church. The great creeds of Christendom (Apostles', Nicene, Athanasian) contain carefully worded statements about the person of Christ. So do the writings of the early church fathers and Dr. Martin Luther. These doctrinal statements contain what have become the technical, theological expressions that Bible-believing Christians use to describe the divine-human person of Christ. Many of these expressions are not used in Scripture itself. But they clearly summarize scriptural teaching. We use them as teaching and learning tools. But it is important to know that all the teachings concerning Christ, as well as everything else that Christians believe, were known and believed long before the church's teachers, councils, and creeds coined the expressions we now use to describe them.

The teaching of the Bible

Christians believe that there are two natures in Christ because the Bible teaches that the eternal Son of God became a man through a miracle of the Holy Spirit in the womb of the virgin Mary. Throughout the New Testament, Jesus presents himself as the Son of God and Son of Man. The Bible teaches that Christ has all the characteristics of God together with a true human nature. The Lord of glory was crucified to pay the ransom price for human sins, then he rose again. Though our human reason cannot possibly begin to grasp it all, we, like the apostle Paul, confess in humble amazement, "Beyond all question, the mystery of godliness is great: He appeared in a body, was vindicated by the Spirit, was seen by angels, was preached among the nations, was believed on in the world, was taken up in glory" (1 Timothy 3:16).

Scripture places great emphasis on the divinity of Jesus. Jesus himself tells us that the words of Peter's confession: "You are the Christ, the Son of the living God" (Matthew 16:16) are the rock, the solid foundation, on which the church is built (verse 18). On this truth the Christian church has continued to stand firm in every age in the face of countless errors and false teachings. Denials that Jesus is truly God have been and continue to be frequent and vehement. They began in Jesus' own day and continue to our own. But the Bible consistently identifies Jesus as "the Son of the living God," the second person of the eternal Trinity.

Both Old and New Testaments ascribe to him the same divine essence, divine characteristics, and divine actions they ascribe to God the Father. Old Testament passages like Psalm 2:7 speak of an eternal Father-Son relationship. Psalm 110 speaks about the coming Messiah as David's "Lord," who would rule everything at the Father's "right hand" and serve as a priest "forever." The Old Testament prophet Isaiah foretold a time in human history when the one who was true God from all eternity would take on a human nature (Isaiah 9:6). Just before Jesus came into the world, an angel told his mother, Mary, "The holy one to be born will be called the Son of God" (Luke 1:35). Numerous New Testament passages say that Jesus helped create the universe in the beginning (John 1:3; Colossians 1:16; Hebrews 1:2).

Jesus' own statement in John 10:30, "I and the Father are one," expresses more than the idea that the Son is similar to the Father in thought and will. It refers to a unity of essence. "Of one being with the Father," the Nicene Creed says of Jesus.[2] The Father and the Son are one in essence, power, mind, thought, and operation. Jesus is not a God of lesser rank. Nor is he a human being who was somehow elevated to the status of God. He is more than a son of God as we by faith are sons of God. Jesus is God in exactly the same way as the Father is God.

The Scripture's testimony that Jesus is God is simply overwhelming. Scripture passages that refer to Jesus' divinity can be divided into a number of groupings: those that directly call him God; those that refer to him as the one and only Son of God; those that ascribe to him divine characteristics; those that reveal his divine works, especially his miracles; and those that ascribe to him divine honor and glory.

Any number of passages could be chosen as representative proof passages for Jesus' divinity. The apostle John in 1 John 5:20 gives Jesus divine names, calling him the "true God and eternal life." In Romans 9:5, Paul refers to Jesus as "God over all, forever praised!" Hebrews 13:8 ascribes to Jesus the divine characteristics of unchangeableness and eternity, speaking of him as "the same yesterday and today and forever." In his Great Commission to his disciples in Matthew 28:18-20, Jesus speaks of his divine authority and his omnipresence: "Surely I am with you always, to the very end of the age" (verse 20). All four gospels record many of Jesus' divine works. His miracles show power over nature, power over sickness and disease, even power over death. All of the gospels record the greatest of all the miracles, Jesus' own resurrection. And in John 5:23, Jesus claims divine honor and glory for himself. He urges all to "honor the Son just as they honor the Father." Two entire books of the New Testament, the gospel of John and the epistle to the Hebrews, have the divinity of Jesus as their themes. And the book of Revelation constantly lifts our eyes of faith to Jesus as the exalted Lamb, the eternally exalted King of kings and Lord of lords.

During his earthly ministry, Jesus also revealed himself as God by the way he taught. Those who heard him realized that Jesus taught with a unique authority (Matthew 7:28,29). There was a marked difference between Jesus' teaching and that of the Old Testament prophets. The prophets presented themselves only as God's spokesmen. Jesus came asserting his authority as God himself. He claimed authority over the temple (Matthew 12:6), the Sabbath (Matthew 12:8), and Satan (Matthew 12:22-29). He exercised the divine prerogative of forgiving sins (Matthew 9:2). He claimed a knowledge of the Father that no one else had and a relationship to the Father that no one else possessed (John 5:19,20). Jesus' great "I am" statements in John's gospel (for example, John 6:35, "I am the bread of life," and John 10:14, "I am the good shepherd") are reminiscent of God's identification of himself to Old Testament believers as the great "I AM," the eternal One (Exodus 3:14). Even Jesus' enemies recognized these and other statements as clear claims of his divinity (John 10:33).

There are other witnesses to Jesus' divinity recorded for us in the Scriptures. The most important witness is God the Father himself. At Jesus' baptism, the Father declared in a voice from heaven, "This is my Son, whom I love; with him I am well pleased" (Matthew 3:17). This Son is the great offspring of the woman promised to Adam and Eve soon after the fall (Genesis 3:15). The apostle Paul shows the connection between prophecy and fulfillment and identifies Jesus as God's eternal Son in Galatians 4:4: "When the time had fully come, God sent his Son, born of a woman." At Jesus' transfiguration, an event that in itself gave visible evidence of his divinity, the Father again declared, "This is my Son" (Matthew 17:5). Likewise the testimony of the disciples, who not only saw Jesus' baptism and the transfiguration but heard his words and witnessed his works, refutes all speculation that Jesus is only a man or a myth. The more these men walked and talked with Jesus, the more the Spirit of God enabled them to understand that he is indeed the Christ, the Son of the living God.

Since the divine essence is one, no answer that satisfies human reason can be given to the question of how only the Son, not the Father or the Holy Spirit, became true man and the substitute for sinners by taking on human nature at God's appointed time in history. But on the basis of Scripture's testimony, we can be absolutely certain of two things: only the Son became human in the fullness of time; and in that Son of God, Jesus Christ, not merely a part but all the fullness of the Godhead dwells. Luther followed Scripture when he wrote, "Christ is a different Person (from the Father). But though He is not the Father, He is still the Creator of heaven and earth, has the divine essence and nature, and was thereafter in time also born of the Virgin Mary; yet there are not two Christs or Sons, but one Jesus."[3]

False teachings

Given all these witnesses to the full divinity of Christ, we might wonder why anyone would question or deny this teaching. But the devil knows how central to our Christian faith and to each individual's salvation the teachings concerning Jesus and his person are. That is why, from the time our Savior himself walked this earth until our own day, Satan has directed his fiercest and most clever attacks at those doctrines that concern Christ, particularly at the teachings concerning the person and divine nature of Christ. Jesus' enemies among the Jews called him a madman. They convicted him as a blasphemer for telling the truth that he is indeed true God, and they condemned him to death. Today Judaism, Buddhism, Islam, and all other heathen religions deny that Jesus is God. We would expect that. Infinitely more dangerous, however, are the attacks on Christ's person that Satan has stirred up within the Christian church itself. Tragically, the history of Christianity is littered with accounts of how false teachers have twisted and misrepresented the Bible's teachings concerning the person of Christ. And many ancient false teachings, though they may appear in slightly different forms, still plague the church today.

Some of these false teachings could be described as *unitarian*. They acknowledge that Jesus is *called* God. But in spite of that, they deny he *is* God. Others are *subordinationist* teachings, which claim that Christ is God but not in the same way the Father is God. In the first century, a man named Cerinthus taught that Jesus was only a man, the son of Joseph and Mary, and that the "divine being" descended on Jesus at his baptism and left him again before he suffered and died. One ancient heretical sect were the Ebionites. Like the Judaizers whom the apostle Paul condemns in Galatians, the Ebionites taught that believers were still bound by the Old Testament laws of Moses. They also taught a "reduced" doctrine of the person of Christ. They too held that Jesus was only a human son of Joseph and

Mary. They recognized him as the promised Messiah but did not accept the truth that he is God. They believed that Jesus became the Christ by keeping the law and that other human beings could raise themselves to divinity by doing the same. They saw Jesus as a teacher and an example rather than as the Messiah, the divine Savior.

As a group, the Ebionites passed rather quickly from the scene of history. But their error, the denial of Christ's divinity and the emphasis on his example rather than his substitutionary atonement, continues in many forms. Today Ebionite thinking is represented by, among others, Christian Science, which teaches that Jesus was a human being who best presented the ideal, our example rather than our all-sufficient Savior.

The application of human reason to the Bible's teaching of the Trinity brought about the ancient false teaching that came to be known as *monarchianism*. After the Greek and Roman philosophers discredited the notion that heaven was filled with many gods, some Christian teachers felt that they somehow had to explain that the worship of the Trinity was the worship of one God, not three. But trying to explain a divine mystery with human logic always results in human errors. Monarchianism denied the full divinity of Christ. *Adoptionist Monarchians* maintained that Jesus was God only in the sense that a power or influence of God rested on him. Jesus was a man, they taught, in whom God's power was particularly active. Because he faithfully made use of that power, he was adopted as God's Son. *Modal Monarchians* taught that God was not three persons, but one person, who took on different forms or roles (modes) of existence as the occasion required. It was actually the Father, they taught, who suffered and died in the "mode" of the Son.

One Monarchian teacher whose false teachings exerted a great deal of influence was Paul of Samosata. Paul lived in the third century, but the influence of his teachings continued long after his death. He denied the virgin birth and the eternity of Christ. Instead, he taught that from the time of Jesus' conception and birth the divine "Logos," or essence, the "eternal Word" (John calls Jesus "the Word" in chapter 1 of his gospel) rested on the human Jesus. That made Jesus an extraordinary man, unlike any other. According to Paul of Samosata, Jesus had the power of divine thought and used it faithfully. But he remained a man. Paul's teaching also emphasized Christ's example and encouraged people to try to save themselves by living like Christ. The Augsburg Confession (1530) specifically condemns the errors of the Samosatenes (Article I). Some sixteenth-century reformers who came after Luther (particularly the Socinians) taught, as did the Samosatenes, that Jesus was a man endowed with great gifts. He employed those gifts so well that eventually divine honor was bestowed on him.

Another false teaching concerning Christ's person that, in one way or another, has troubled the church throughout the New Testament age is Arianism. Arius was a fourth-century churchman, a native of Alexandria in Egypt. He was a pupil of Lucian (died 311) who, in turn, had been influenced by Paul of Samosata. Arius believed that Jesus existed prior to his incarnation. But he also taught that the Son was not eternal. According to Arius, Jesus was a created being who did not share the substance or essence of God. He was a personal being intermediate between God and man, greater than any other creature but, nevertheless, not eternal. There was a time, Arian theology held, when Jesus did not exist. His incarnation

(incarnation can be defined as Jesus' "taking on of human nature" by virtue of his conception and birth) did not bring union between the human and the divine. Jesus came into our world to save mankind by revealing the will of God and calling people to repentance and obedience. It was the Arian Controversy that brought about the Council of Nicaea in 325. There the church responded to the errors of Arius by setting forth in creedal form the Bible's teaching that Jesus is "God from God, Light from Light, true God from true God, begotten, not made, of one being with the Father,"[4] who at a time appointed by God took on our nature and became fully human.

Arianism was condemned by the Council of Nicaea in 325. It was condemned again by the Council of Constantinople in 381 and by the Council of Chalcedon in 451. But like so many heresies and false teachings, Arianism has reared its ugly head time and again and still continues to trouble the church into the third Christian millennium. Today the Jehovah's Witnesses teach that though Jesus is the Son of God, he is inferior to the Father. He was a created being who became solely human and whose body was destroyed at death. The Mormons teach that Jesus is not the only-begotten, eternal Son of God but a man who became God, just as we too can become gods. The "Jesus Seminar," a group of two hundred contemporary scholars who meet regularly to study the gospels and try to discover their "real meaning," has concluded that Jesus never claimed to be God and probably spoke fewer than half the sayings attributed to him in the New Testament. Yet another theologian who calls himself Lutheran has written, "The notion of the preexistent Son of God becoming a human being in the womb of a virgin and then returning to his heavenly home is bound up with a mythological picture of the world that clashes with our modern, scientific world view."[5] That view of Christ, unfortunately, is being taught in many prominent Lutheran seminaries, guaranteeing that confusion concerning the person of Christ will continue to plague the church well into the future.

The Unitarian movement also denies Jesus' divinity. Unitarianism had its origin in Europe in the sixteenth century and found its way to America in the eighteenth century. Unitarians reject the doctrine of the Trinity. They claim to worship only the Father as God and teach that Jesus is only a man. Like the Socinians, Unitarians make reason the supreme guide in matters of faith. The Unitarian movement itself never became a powerful force in the religious world. But Unitarian thought, especially the rejection of all that does not seem "reasonable," has become firmly entrenched in many so-called mainline Christian denominations in America. The result is almost continual attacks on scriptural teachings that are the key to a clear confession of Jesus' divinity—including the virgin birth, the miracles, and Jesus' bodily resurrection. Cults like scientology, the New Age Movement, and the Unification Church all view Jesus not as "God from God" but as a "godly" human being.

Denials of the eternal deity of Jesus take many forms. But generally they are prompted by two things: human logic says it is impossible for God and man to be united in one person, and human pride says that human beings are capable of earning heaven and satisfying God's just demands by things that they can do. This is precisely, however, why the teaching that Jesus is the eternal Son of God is so important and so precious to Bible-believing Christians. If Jesus were only a good man and a model of virtue, he could no more save us than any of those other good men to whom the world often compares him. If that is true, our sins would still be our responsibility. God, in his perfect justice, would still charge a person's sins to each individual. And we would never be able to escape the punishment that we deserve for those sins. A purely human Christ could never be our Savior, our Redeemer. But how blessedly comforting and refreshing for you and me and every other guilty sinner is the Bible's central assurance: God's own eternal Son loved me and gave himself for me! He and he alone could and did deal with my sin, my guilt, my punishment, and my curse. *God's Son* has made me free.

2

Jesus Christ Is True Man

From all eternity Jesus has existed as God, in a timeless and unique relationship with the Father and the Spirit in the Holy Trinity. There was never a time when Jesus did not exist, never a time when he was not true God. But at the precise moment in time determined in the eternal counsels of the Holy Trinity, Jesus also took on a true human nature like our own. He was conceived as a human child in the womb of the virgin Mary. Thus, without ceasing to be God, Jesus also became and continues to be fully human. All that Scripture says and teaches about Jesus after that singular moment in time in which he "became incarnate," or took on a true human nature, it says and teaches about the unique person who is the God-man.

The teaching of the Bible

Just as clearly as it teaches Christ's true divinity, the Bible also teaches his true and perfect humanity. In passages like 1 Timothy 2:5 ("the man Christ Jesus") and John 8:40 ("a man who has told you the truth"), the inspired writers directly call Jesus a man. The Jews never doubted that the Jesus who lived and moved among them was a true human being. Nor did the evangelists, who recorded the story of his life on earth. One of the expressions Jesus used most frequently to refer to himself was "Son of Man." And in his great comparison of Adam and Christ in Romans chapter 5, Paul refers to Jesus as the second Adam. Just like the first Adam, Jesus is a true human being, with a human body and soul. He was not, as some have speculated, a "phantom man," who appeared in a body that was not real. Jesus' body is not a spiritual body, totally different from ours. The Athanasian Creed sets forth clear scriptural truth when it says of Jesus, "He is man, born in time from the nature of his mother, . . . fully man, with rational soul and human flesh."[6]

As Jesus is the one and only Son of his heavenly Father according to his divine nature, he is also a descendant of the patriarchs, the father-leaders of Israel, according to his human nature (Romans 9:5). He is Abraham's Seed (Galatians 3:16-19) and David's Branch (Jeremiah 23:5). Jesus did not bring a human nature down with him from heaven. He received it from his Israelite ancestors, many of whom are mentioned in the genealogies of Matthew chapter 1 and Luke chapter 3. Jesus received his human nature specifically from his mother as the "fruit" of Mary's womb (Luke 1:42 KJV). The Scriptures also refer to various aspects of Christ's human nature, including his body (Matthew 26:12), his flesh and bones (Luke 24:39), his soul (Matthew 26:38), and his human emotions and will (John 11:35).

As it presents the human side of the God-man to us, the Bible gives Jesus human names, including Mary's son (Mark 6:3) and the Son of Man (John 1:51). It reveals him to us as one who displayed all the characteristics and activities of human nature as we know it but without sin. Jesus was conceived and born, he grew, he was hungry and thirsty, he ate and drank, he slept and wept, he suffered and died. The Bible also shows us how completely Jesus placed his human body and soul into the service of his redemptive work. Saint Matthew's account of Jesus' passion and death, beginning at chapter 26:30, gives us a revealing and moving portrait of the physical suffering the God-man endured for us. His human soul experienced sorrow (26:38) as the weight of the world's sins descended on him. He willingly subjected his human will to the heavenly Father's divine will (26:42). He suffered the humiliation of mockery, shameful treatment, and unjust condemnation (26:65-67). He endured the dreadful physical anguish of flogging (27:26) and died a criminal's death of crucifixion (27:35). He endured the spiritual pangs of the eternal separation from God that is hell (27:46).

Without a human nature, without a rational soul and will, Jesus could not have carried out his atoning work in accord with God's divine plan, which called for a perfect substitute to live, die, and rise again in the sinners' place. The ancient church teachers put it well when they stated, *"Quod Filius Dei non assunsit, non redemit"* [What the Son of God did not assume, he did not redeem].[7] That is why, since the days of the apostles, the church has understood the importance of confessing the true humanity as well as the true divinity of Christ. Both are necessary for him to be our Redeemer. An early Lutheran catechism stated it clearly and eloquently: "It was necessary for Him to be a man that He might suffer and die; but as no mere man could bear the sin of the human race, together with the wrath of God and the curse of the Law, nor satisfy infinite divine justice, nor overcome death, hell, and the devil, it was necessary that He should at the same time be true God."[8]

A description of Jesus' human nature

If Jesus is a true human being like ourselves, yet at the same time true God, we legitimately ask, "What is his human nature like?" We have already seen that it is similar to our own in that Jesus experienced all of human life. Jesus assumed a human nature, not as Adam possessed it before the fall but with the limitations and needs that are common to human beings since the fall. No, Jesus didn't assume the sin that is passed down to every human being born into our world in the natural way since the fall. A distinction must be made between human nature itself and the original, or inherited, sin that clings to it. But in his state of humiliation, which we shall study in greater detail in a later chapter, Jesus assumed the weaknesses and limitations that are the consequences of sin in this sinful world without assuming the sin itself. The evangelists tell us that he experienced hunger, thirst, and fatigue. Things that he saw and experienced troubled him and made him sad. He became a "man of sorrows, and familiar with suffering," in accord with the ancient prophecy of Isaiah 53:3. Yet Jesus did not assume personal diseases or defects such as leprosy or other terminal illnesses, which would have prematurely shortened his life.

Just because Jesus is the God-man, there are certain significant differences between his humanity and ours. All other human beings derive their nature by physical descent from sinful human parents (John 3:6). The result is that all are sinners from the moment of their conception (Psalm 51:5). Jesus' human nature, however, came into existence through the operation and work of the Holy Spirit in the womb of a virgin. This one-of-a-kind miracle enabled Jesus to take on our humanity without inheriting our sin. Throughout his lifetime Jesus remained free from sin. Jesus' sinlessness and his attendant sinless humanity were necessary for him to accomplish our salvation. Only to "a lamb without blemish or defect" (1 Peter 1:19) could the Father charge the guilt of all the world as a substitute. The reason that Christ was sinless was not some mysterious preservation of a sinless seed in Israel. It was surely not the sinlessness of Mary, who proclaimed herself a sinner and in need of a Savior even after she was told that she would have the unique honor of giving birth to God's Son, the world's Savior (Luke 1:47). Nor was Jesus a sinner from birth who somehow evolved to perfection. But the Holy Spirit's miracle of divine grace and omnipotence preserved Christ from taking on human sin when he took on our human nature. By this miracle he was "set apart from sinners" (Hebrews 7:26).

In considering the sinlessness of Jesus' humanity, it is also important for us to remember that from the very moment it came into existence, Christ's human nature belonged to the person of the Son of God. By virtue of his divine nature, Jesus was sinless and incapable of sin. Yet, as the God-man, he was truly tempted and tried but only from the outside, not from the inside as we are.

Because Christ's human nature is sinless, it is immortal. He died, not because death was natural to him, as it is to us, but because he willed himself to die. His voluntary giving up of his sinless life gave his death redemptive value for us.

The Bible tells us nothing about the physical appearance of Jesus. It doesn't even hint that it was different from that of any of his contemporaries. This is no doubt due to the fact that in his state of humiliation, he relinquished not only the full and constant use of his divine glory but also the unique privileges of a sinless humanity. Jesus blended into the human scene of which he voluntarily became a part. He chose to appear not as Adam appeared before the fall but as Adam and his descendants appeared after the fall.

Jesus' human nature, though distinct from his divine nature, was "assumed" into the divine person at the moment of conception. This means that, although Jesus possesses two natures, he possesses only one personality. Though he has a true human body and soul, his human nature never existed apart from his divine nature. And it is the divine nature that gives the God-man his personality.

From the moment he was conceived by the Holy Spirit's miracle in the virgin's womb, therefore, Jesus has been and continues to be the God-man. Not only as a baby in his mother's arms but also as an adolescent and mature man, Jesus possessed a truly human and a truly divine nature. The fact that the God-man passed through every stage of human life and development is an essential part of his substitutionary work for us. In the eternal God-man, we have a High Priest who meets our needs in every way (Hebrews 7:26). Knowing his person lays the foundation for understanding his work and for appreciating the greatness and completeness of our salvation. And knowing that he still retains the human nature that experienced everything we experience and personally understands our needs gives us the courage to "approach the throne of grace with confidence, so that we may receive mercy and find grace to help us in our time of need" (Hebrews 4:16).

False teachings

Just as human teachings that question or deny what Scripture teaches concerning the divinity of Christ have troubled individual believers and the church from the days of the apostles, there are also countless false teachings concerning what the Bible teaches about Jesus' true humanity. In a book on the great confessions of the church, which he wrote in 1538, Martin Luther clearly recognized both as the devil's strategy. Luther observed that the devil "attacks Christ in three lines of battle. One will not let him be God, another will not let him be man, and the third will not let him do what he has done. Each of the three wants to reduce Christ to nothing."[9] Luther's words were based on a thorough study of history and a careful observation of the religious scene in the sixteenth century. His remarks certainly hold true today. In the previous chapter we considered ancient and modern false teachings that attack Christ's divinity, teachings that will not let Christ be God. Here we consider ancient and modern false teachings that will not let him be man.

Scripture clearly teaches that in addition to being true God, Jesus is also, from the moment of his incarnation, a true human being with flesh and blood, body and soul. In the early church, those who rejected the Bible's teachings concerning Jesus' true humanity were called Docetists, from the Greek word meaning "to appear." Docetism was not really a formulated or unified system of teaching or doctrine. The word *Docetist* was applied to all who, in one way or another, considered the humanity and the sufferings of an earthly Christ as apparent rather than real. Forms of Docetism ranged from the religious philosophy which taught that Christ was a phantom without a real human body (Gnosticism) to the idea that Christ miraculously escaped the shame and suffering of the cross by having Judas Iscariot or Simon of Cyrene change places with him just before the crucifixion. Docetists taught, for example, that when Jesus and his disciples walked along the Sea of Galilee, 12—not 13—sets of footprints appeared in the sand.

The idea of Christ as a phantom being doesn't appear to be too popular today, although there are surely those who hold it. The world today, however, has more sophisticated forms of what we could refer to as Docetism. Inspired by modern man's refusal to accept anything contrary to the laws of science or the dictates of human reason, modern "Docetists" not only question the humanity of Christ, they question his very existence as the gospels present it. There may have been a historical figure named Jesus, they allow. But he was nothing like the evangelists portray him. In fact, these present-day teachers would have us believe there is very little we can know about the "historical Jesus."

Ancient Docetists said that Jesus only seemed to be a human being. He only seemed to suffer, die, and rise again. Modern religious thought holds that the early church—the "primitive Christian community"—became overly enthused about Jesus. The result of this enthusiasm was that they taught others not who Jesus really was but who he seemed to them to be. According to this theory, the early Christians, especially the disciples, expressed their beliefs about Jesus in mythological terms and figurative language. Modern Docetists (we could also call them modern Gnostics) teach that there was no real physical resurrection. There could be no such thing, because it is contrary to natural laws. But Jesus and his teachings made such a great impression on his disciples that it seemed to them he continued to live among them, even after he had died. This "phantom Christ" invented by the disciples became a hero of legends involving supernatural, miraculous things. The truth that in Christ Jesus God took on a human nature like our own and that the gospels bring us factual history is vigorously denied. Paul Tillich, a twentieth-century German-American theologian who dared to call himself Lutheran, declared that "the assertion that 'God has become man' is not a paradoxical but a nonsensical statement."[10]

If Jesus is not the God-man, then who is he? Most modern Gnostics would answer, "We know what he isn't; but we really don't know for sure who he is." Some have even questioned whether a man named Jesus, as the gospels describe him, ever walked this earth. Albert Schweitzer, the well-known humanitarian and modernist theologian, published a study titled *The Quest of the Historical Jesus*.[11] Rudolf Bultmann, another twentieth-century German theologian, claimed that the gospels aren't really history. The supposedly mythical worldview they present is a thing of the past. All we can know, Bultmann suggested, is the "that ness" of Jesus—whatever *that ness* means.[12] So today's theologians haven't come much further than first-century Docetists and Gnostics, who taught a "phantom Christ." Recently a contemporary German Lutheran theologian admitted that the historical figure of Jesus existed but that "modern science has also shown us that this [information we possess about Jesus] is not sufficient to write a biography of Jesus" and that the gospel accounts were not written as historical narratives but "with the intention of showing how important and significant Jesus is."[13] A theologian in the Evangelical Lutheran Church in America says the gospels are "filled with theological claims and confessions . . . which go far beyond the objective events of the history of Jesus."[14]

These modern denials of the historicity of Christ and the accuracy of the Bible may very well be the greatest challenge the enemies of biblical Christianity have ever posed. If the Bible is no longer considered God's inspired and inerrant message to mankind, there are no final answers about Jesus or, for that matter, about anything. Throughout history the visible church has, by God's grace, survived many false teachings. But a church that claims to be Christian yet declares the central events in the life of Christ to be myths and not factual history will surely destroy itself. May God preserve us all in a clear confession of Christ, a confession that Jesus is truly God and truly man as the Holy Scriptures portray him.

3

The Virgin Birth

"He is God, eternally begotten from the nature of the Father, and he is man, born in time from the nature of his mother, fully God, fully man."[15] With these words the Athanasian Creed speaks of the twofold generation of the God-man. As true God, Jesus has always existed in a divine Father-Son relationship to God the Father. This relationship is not like any father-son relationship here on earth. It is not a relationship in which the son is subordinate to the father. Nor is it a relationship in which the father preceded the son. Eternal Son of the Father is Scripture's description to us human beings of the timeless relationship that exists between the Father and the Son in the mysterious union of the Holy Trinity. Our human minds cannot grasp or understand it. What is clear, however, is that there was never a time that Jesus did not exist as the Son, coequal and coeternal with the Father. There was never a time when he was not God (John 1:1,2).

There was, however, a time when Jesus was not a man. It was not in eternity but in time, at the time appointed by God and definable in terms of human history, that for us and for our salvation, Jesus took on a true human nature in addition to the divine nature he possessed from eternity. The taking on of a human nature by the second person of God is known as the *incarnation*. The incarnation of the Son of God was a miraculous act of God in connection with the carrying out of his plan for mankind's salvation. The way God carried out this miracle is stated in the Apostles' Creed: He "was conceived by the Holy Spirit, born of the virgin Mary." Through his miraculous conception and birth, Jesus, without ceasing to be God, became a true human being like ourselves yet without sin. The marvelous manner in which God's Son took on our nature and entered our world was at the same time an awesome act of his almighty power and an amazing act of humiliation. Christians from the first century to our own day have always regarded the teaching of Christ's incarnation as a mystery no less profound than that of the doctrine of the Trinity itself.

The eternal Son of God became incarnate by a miracle of the Holy Spirit and entered our world by means of the virgin birth. What do we mean by the term *virgin birth*? Simply stated, the doctrine of the virgin birth is that Jesus had a human mother but no human father. Though he was born in the natural way, his conception was supernatural. According to the laws of nature, it takes a male and a female and a union between the sperm and the egg of the two to produce a child. The conception of Jesus, however, was not the result of a physical union between a man and a woman at all (Matthew 1:18). Though still physically a virgin, Mary became a mother (Matthew 1:23). So Jesus derived his humanity from Mary, though not in the normal way. When the angel brought Mary the startling announcement that she would become a mother, Mary did not understand how this could happen. The angel told her, "The Holy Spirit will come upon you, and the power of the Most High will overshadow you" (Luke 1:35). To puzzled Joseph, who at first could only conclude that Mary had been unfaithful to him, the angel explained that Mary's child had not been conceived in human unfaithfulness. The conception had been a miracle brought about by the power of the Holy Spirit (Matthew 1:20).

The accounts in Matthew and Luke that refer to Christ's conception and birth are supported by other passages in Scripture. The apostle Paul directs us back to the prophecies of Genesis and Isaiah when he declares, "God sent his Son, born of a woman" (Galatians 4:4). If Paul had known of an earthly father, first-century custom would have dictated that he mention the father. Instead, the expression "born of a woman" stands out as extraordinary. Whenever Jesus speaks about himself, he speaks of an earthly mother and a heavenly Father. The only one he calls Father is his Father in heaven. As a 12-year-old child, Jesus spoke about his "Father's house," the temple. There the heavenly Father revealed his presence and his Word was taught. In John chapter 6, when the Jews referred to him as Joseph's son, Jesus emphatically declared that he is the Son of God. He speaks of the heavenly Father as the one with whom he enjoys a unique, eternal relationship: "The Father is in me, and I in the

Father" (John 10:38). And when he says, "I and the Father are one" (verse 30), he claims a relationship with his heavenly Father that no human son can claim with an earthly father.

Few teachings of Scripture are denied as frequently and defiantly as the doctrine of Christ's virgin birth. The general assumption is that because it is contrary to nature and to reason, this doctrine is impossible for reasonable people to accept. Skeptics denied it in the first century. Skeptics have denied it ever since and continue to deny it today. Even in some Lutheran circles, Christ's virgin birth is emphatically denied. Present-day theologians, who piously insist that they are searching for the "historical Jesus" as opposed to the "exaggerated picture of Jesus" they believe the gospels paint, declare that the doctrine of the virgin birth is not part of the church's proclamation. Accounts of the virgin birth in Matthew and Luke, they tell us, were borrowed from Greek mythology to try to explain the importance of Jesus to the Christian community. So who do these scholars claim that Jesus was? And how did he really come into the world? Most regard him as the son of Joseph and Mary at best, an illegitimate son of Mary at worst. And none regard him as the Christ, the Son of God.

The teaching of the virgin birth is important for a proper understanding of Jesus' person. If Jesus had simply been an offspring of Joseph and Mary, or of Mary and some other human father, a Roman soldier perhaps, he would no more be the Son of God than any other human child. That's why those who deny the divinity of Christ so vehemently deny the virgin birth. And those who deny his virgin birth deny his divinity. As Jesus' resurrection serves as a divinely designated sign of God's approval of what he did, the virgin birth is the divinely designated sign of approval of who he is. Together these serve as foundational truths for the faith that confesses, "I believe that Jesus Christ, true God, begotten of the Father from all eternity, and also true man, born of the virgin Mary, is my Lord. He has redeemed me, . . ."[16]

Could Jesus have come into the world in another way? While it is presumptuous to speculate on what God can and does do, the fact that God chose the virgin birth is significant and necessary because he did choose it. By the virgin birth, God brought his Son into the world without the taint of original sin. And he enabled him to serve each of us as the perfect substitute, the "one mediator between God and men, the man Christ Jesus, who gave himself as a ransom for all men—the testimony given in its proper time" (1 Timothy 2:5,6). Jesus' miraculous birth corresponds with his marvelous life, his wondrous works, and his amazing exaltation—all undertaken *for us!* It is true; the Bible leaves no doubt. The eternal Son of God took on a true human nature and was conceived by the Holy Spirit and born of the virgin Mary for us. The angels marveled at that wondrous miracle. And so do we!

4

The Personal Union

"The Son of God in the fullness of time joined to himself, in a perpetual union which shall not be dissolved for all eternity, a true human nature, true, complete, entire, of the same substance as ours, possessing a body and a rational soul which contain within themselves all the conditions, desires, powers and faculties proper to and characteristic of human nature."[17] With this rather lengthy and technical sentence the sixteenth-century Lutheran theologian Martin Chemnitz summarized the contents of the first three chapters of this book. He stated that in Jesus Christ there are two separate and distinct natures—the divine and the human. The relationship of these two natures to each other, and the fact that they are joined as they are in one divine-human person, is absolutely unique. Jesus' divine nature and his human nature, joined at his conception by a miracle of the Holy Spirit, are inseparable from each other. Yet each nature retains its own essential properties and characteristics. The two natures in Christ are not combined or commingled to form a third nature. They are not simply "glued together" so that individual functions of each can be distinguished. Nor are there two Christs; there is only one Christ. Learning what the Scriptures say about the relationship to each other of the two natures he possesses is an important element in our study of the person of Christ. A proper understanding of Scripture helps us identify and reject the many false teachings about Christ's person that continue to trouble the church.

The relationship of the two natures

The intimate union of the two natures in Christ, divine and human, in the one person of the God-man is called the *personal union*. Theologians also refer to it as the hypostatic union, from a Greek word that means "person." This union was effected when the second person of the eternal Trinity assumed a human nature into his divine person. As a result of that union, God and man are forever one undivided, indivisible person in Christ. This is the great "mystery of godliness," about which Paul speaks in 1 Timothy 3:16, when in awe he exclaims, "He [Christ] appeared in a body."

As we ponder this "mystery of godliness," it is important for us to understand that Christ's divine nature was the *assuming* nature and his human nature, the *assumed* nature. There was never a time when the divine nature did not exist. There was never a time when Jesus did not exist as true God. But at God's appointed time in human history the eternal Son of God received and incorporated into his person a true human nature. We call this moment in time Christ's incarnation. Christ did not assume the human nature into his divine person in such a way that there are two persons or two Christs. But as a result of his assuming the human nature into his divine person, Jesus Christ is now one person with two distinct natures. He is at the same time both God and man.

At no time did Jesus' human nature exist apart from the divine nature. From its beginning, Christ's human nature had its existence, and for all eternity it will have its existence, in the person of the fully divine and fully human Son of God. Christ's human nature is, nevertheless, very real and personal. It consists, as does every human nature, of a true human body and soul. The union of the two natures in Christ, however, is so intimate and inseparable that neither nature can be conceived of without or apart from the other. At the same time, however, each of the two natures retains its own character and peculiarities, unmixed with the other. The divine nature retains its omniscience, omnipotence, omnipresence, and all of the other divine qualities. The human nature retains its capacity to walk, talk, eat, sleep, be locally circumscribed, and feel emotions.

Two natures, yet one person, unmixed but inseparably united. In all of human experience there is really nothing to which we can compare the union of the divine and human natures in Christ. No illustration can ever adequately capture this divine mystery.

Still, the Formula of Concord (1577), perhaps the most thorough and detailed of the historic Lutheran Confessions, provides an illustration that helps us begin to understand the mystery of the personal union. The picture is that of iron heated by fire. As the heating process takes place, neither the iron nor the fire is changed in its basic essence. But the fire penetrates and permeates the iron. The heated iron becomes warm and glows. In the same way Jesus' assuming nature, the divine nature, permeates and penetrates the assumed human nature so that both natures constitute one divine-human person.[18] Yes, it defies human logic. No, it cannot be adequately explained by human pictures. But everything the Bible says and teaches about the second person of the eternal Trinity after he assumed a human nature, it says and teaches, not just about one nature, but about one God-man, our Savior.

That such a personal union exists is clearly taught by Scripture. Countless passages testify that in the incarnate Christ, God is man and man is God. Matthew 16:13-17 reveals that the Son of Man is at the same time the Son of the living God. Luke 1:32,33 calls the Son of Mary the Son of the Most High. Romans 9:5 declares that Christ, who is a physical descendant of the fathers of the Jewish nation, is at the same time "God over all, forever praised!" And John 1:14 tells us, "The Word became flesh." The Word (Greek, *Logos*) is John's special title for the second person of the Trinity. Jesus is "the Word" because he is God's ultimate revelation of himself to mankind. God's gospel message of grace and truth is embodied in Jesus. Jesus makes God known to us, and to know Jesus is to know God. The Word, John tells us, the eternally existing Logos, became flesh. He didn't change his divine nature or stop being God. Later in that same verse, John writes, "We have seen his glory, the glory of the One and Only, who came from the Father, full of grace and truth." At the same time flesh denotes a complete human being, with both body and soul.

These passages and others like them lead us to an inescapable conclusion. From the time the eternal Word assumed flesh, the flesh is not without the Word and the Word is not without the flesh. Wherever the one nature is, there is the other. Whatever the one nature does, the other nature shares in doing as well. The two natures are inseparable, yet distinct. In the words of the Definition of Chalcedon of A.D. 451, the two natures are "without confusion, change, division, or separation." The act of the eternal Logos in taking on a human nature was momentary. The resulting state is eternal. And the Christ who redeemed us and the Christ we worship is not just the Logos separate from the assumed nature. Nor was or is he ever just the assumed flesh outside of the eternal Logos. He is the God-man.

The communion of natures

As they teach a personal union of the two natures in Christ, the Scriptures also teach the "communication" of these natures to each other. By virtue of this communication, or "communion," that which is the property of the divine nature is communicated to the human nature. That which is human is, at the same time, assumed by the divine nature. From passages that speak to this subject, we learn that in the God-man, Christ Jesus, the divine Logos is never outside the human nature. Nor is the human nature outside the Logos. But the divine nature penetrates and permeates the human nature it assumed. And the human nature is at all times and completely filled with the divine. "In Christ," Paul puts it so powerfully in Colossians 2:9, "all the fullness of the Deity lives in bodily form." Christ's human nature—while remaining truly human—participates, by virtue of the communication of natures, in the personal union, not only in those acts that are distinctive to humanity but in all the divine acts, including forgiving and judging. And the divine nature—while remaining truly divine—participates also in those acts that are common to the human nature.

In a rather lengthy and technical quotation that probably needs to be read more than once to be understood, a seventeenth-century Lutheran teacher summed up the communication of natures that belongs to the personal union: "The communion of natures is that most intimate participation and combination of the divine nature of the Logos and the assumed human nature by which the Logos, through a most intimate and profound interpenetration, so permeates, inhabits, and appropriates to himself the human nature personally united with him that from both, mutually intercommunicating, there arises one incommunicable subject, namely, one person."[19]

False teachings

Because they are yet another divine mystery, attempts to fathom or even explain the personal union and the communion of natures in Christ can lead only to errors and false teachings. As with most, if not all, of the divine mysteries concerning the God-man, the church has had to deal with a multitude of such errors. Early in the fifth century a bishop named Nestorius taught that there were two separate persons in the incarnate Christ. One person had a divine nature. The other person had a human nature. Nestorius acknowledged a connection between the two persons but regarded them as completely distinct from each other, like "two boards glued together." In opposing the error of Nestorius, the Council of Chalcedon in 451 declared, "We confess one and the same

Jesus Christ, the Son and Lord only-begotten in two natures, without mixture, without change, *without divisions, without separation.*"[20]

Some of the errors of Nestorius were repeated in the sixteenth century by the Swiss reformer Ulrich Zwingli. Zwingli tried to maintain a separation of the two natures in Christ by trying to distinguish between what each nature could and could not do. Zwingli's Nestorian errors in his Christology led directly to his well-known false views about the Lord's Supper. Because he was convinced that Christ's human nature was locally circumscribed in heaven and therefore could not be present everywhere on earth as the Sacrament is celebrated, he taught, as most Reformed churches still teach today, that Christ's presence is only represented by the bread and the wine in the Lord's Supper. Christ does not truly give communicants his body to eat and his blood to drink in the Sacrament.

Eutyches, another fifth-century teacher and a fervent opponent of Nestorius, erred in the other direction. He taught that the personal union was a mingling of the two natures into each other, so that an entirely new nature came into being. According to Eutyches, in the incarnate Christ there is only one nature, the divine nature. Jesus' human nature was swallowed up into the divine, as droplets of water are swallowed up into the ocean, losing their individual identity.

In rejecting Nestorianism, Eutychianism, and other errors about the personal union, theologians of the early church used various adverbs to describe the permanent uniting of the two natures into one without destroying the essence of either. These adverbs include *unconfoundedly*—the two natures were not mingled into a new, third nature; *unchangeably*—Christ's divine nature was not changed into flesh, nor was flesh changed into divine nature; and *indivisibly* and *inseparably*—the two natures of Christ are never separated by time or space.

In opposition to all ancient and modern errors concerning the personal union, Lutheran theologians have formulated a series of negative statements about what it is not.[21] The personal union is not just a union in name only, as though the Son of Man were only called God. It is not a natural union like that of soul and body, which were created for each other. It cannot be, for this union intimately and inseparably unites the Creator and the creature, God and man, in one person. The personal union is not an accidental or external union, as when two boards are glued together or a human body is dressed in clothing. An accidental union does not join two things into one in the same manner as the personal union unites two natures into one person. The personal union is not a sustaining union by virtue of the divine presence, as God is present in and sustains all creatures. Creatures are not assumed into the Godhead as Christ's human nature was assumed into the person of God. It is not a relative union, which places two things in a certain relationship with each other but leaves them separate in some respect. In Christ, the two natures are inseparably joined by a most intimate and personal union and together constitute the indivisible Christ. It is not an essential or commingling union, by which two natures coalesced into one essence. Both natures are completely present in the divine-human Christ. And it is not a union by adoption. Jesus was not a human being who was adopted by the Father to be his Son. The incarnation was not an adoption of a human person by God but the assumption of Jesus' human nature into the person of God.

To consider the two natures of Christ as separate or to deny the personal union and the communion of natures results in denying the atoning work of Christ. That work could be brought about only by a divine-human person, a God-man. Had Jesus not been true God, he could not have accomplished our salvation. Had he not been true man, he could not have served as the substitute for mankind called for by God's eternal salvation plan. But by virtue of the personal union and the communion of natures, Jesus was and is the perfect answer to God's salvation plan. The God-man alone could and did live and die and rise again to rescue and save a lost and fallen world. Indeed, "the mystery of godliness is great: He appeared in a body, . . ." (1 Timothy 3:16). And in that body, for us and for our salvation, dwells all the fullness of God.

5

The Communion of Properties

As a consequence and result of the personal union of the divine and human natures in Christ, there exists what we referred to in the previous chapter as the "communication, or communion, of natures." This means that in the divine-human Christ, that which is the property of the divine nature is communicated to the human nature and that which is the property of the human nature is assumed by the divine. What is true of the interrelationship of Christ's two natures in general is also true of the individual properties of those natures. They too are communicated to and shared with each other by virtue of the personal union. This sharing of properties is referred to as the "communication, or communion, of idioms." *Idioms* is a technical term for attributes, experiences, and activities peculiar to the divine and human natures in Christ. Sometimes the word *properties* is substituted for *idioms*. A divine idiom or property, for example, would be omnipotence (having all power). A human idiom or property would be experiencing pain.

The study of the communication of idioms, or communion of properties, is a rather difficult one. Because of its complicated nature and highly formal vocabulary, it is not a subject frequently discussed in sermons or even in Bible classes. It is important, however, because it helps us define what Scripture teaches about the relationship of Christ's human and divine characteristics to each other and to his work of salvation. Likewise, a correct understanding of this difficult subject helps us recognize and reject errors that lead to confusion about the person of Christ.

The personal union of the two natures, God and man, in Christ could not be perfect or permanent without the participation of the properties or characteristics (idioms) of both natures in that union. When the Son of God assumed human nature to carry out God's plan for mankind's salvation, he did not give up his divine nature or any of its qualities. At the same time, however, he assumed, together with the human nature he took on, all the properties that belong to that nature. The communion of properties is the participation of all the properties of the divine and human natures in the personal union of the two natures in Jesus, the God-man. These properties include not only the characteristics of each nature but also their activities. The word *communion*, and the concept that lies behind it, is likewise significant. As the two natures in Christ remain separate and distinct in the miraculous union of the divine and the human, each nature retains the properties essential to itself. Yet there is only one Christ. There is only one, single, undivided person.

In order to help us understand the concept of the communion of properties a bit more easily, Lutheran theologians have divided the Bible passages that speak about this subject into three categories, or *genera*, a word meaning "classes" or "kinds." The formal names for the classes of passages that describe the communion of properties are "idiomatic genus," "majestic genus," and "apotelesmatic genus." The terms certainly sound strange to us. They were forged in the heat of controversies largely unknown to us and during a time far removed from us. But this strange-sounding language is typical of the manner in which our Lutheran forefathers sought to safeguard and pass down to us divine truth, especially in regard to this vitally important subject, by using as precise and carefully chosen language as they possibly could. What a Lutheran seminary professor of our own day has said concerning the significance of the three genera can be summed up in this way: The idiomatic genus consists of passages which assure us that Jesus is the God-man; in the majestic genus are passages which show us that in the man Jesus we find God; and in the apotelesmatic genus are passages that reveal Jesus, the God-man, as our kinsman and Redeemer.[22]

The idiomatic genus

The idiomatic genus contains Scripture passages that ascribe properties which are clearly peculiar to the divine nature or the human nature of Christ to the God-man Jesus. These passages remind us that while each nature remains distinct, there is a genuine sharing of each nature's attributes or qualities in the one divine-human person of Christ. Whatever Jesus is and does since taking on the human nature, he is and does as a single person, the God-man. In Acts 3:15, the apostle Peter tells his Jewish listeners, "You killed the author of life." The ability to be killed is peculiar to the human nature. "Author of life" is a clear designation of Jesus as eternally divine. In the abstract, it is not possible to say that God could suffer. But when Scripture says that the rulers of this world "crucified the Lord of glory" (1 Corinthians 2:8), it is saying that God was there on Calvary. So, by virtue of the personal union and communion of properties, we rightly teach that Jesus, the God-man, gave his life for us.

Other examples of the idiomatic genus are found in Hebrews 13:8, where we read, "Jesus Christ is the same yesterday and today and forever"; and in John 8:58, where Jesus declares, "Before Abraham was born, I am!" Jesus is the Lord's human name. Unchangeableness, however, is a divine characteristic. Similarly, in the abstract, it is not possible to say that Jesus' humanity existed from all eternity. But what both passages tell us is that Jesus, who is both God and man in one person, is unchangeable and eternal. There is only one Christ. He is fully human yet, at the same time, fully and completely divine. He was born in time yet does not change; he has no beginning and knows no end. Many other passages as well ascribe characteristics peculiar to one or the other of his two natures to the divine-human Christ. These all remind us that after Jesus' incarnation, even though each nature and its characteristics are separate and distinct, they are now joined in a unique, personal union. And in and by virtue of that union, the characteristics and qualities of both natures can and must be ascribed to Jesus, the God-man.

In every age of Christian church history, false teachers have denied the idiomatic genus by trying to drive a wedge between the divine and human natures of Christ.

Paul of Samosata, whose false teachings concerning Christ's person we have considered in a previous chapter, taught that Jesus was only a uniquely receptive man on whom God was able to exercise his divine influence, a "fit channel" through whom God worked miracles and redeemed humanity. Paul taught that Jesus eventually achieved permanent union with God because of his moral excellence. Nestorius, to whom we also referred previously, refused to acknowledge the personal union brought about by the incarnation. He refused to believe that words like *born, suffered,* and *died,* describing human properties and activities, could be properly ascribed to the Son of God. Nestorius objected to referring to Mary as the mother of God and was uncomfortable with statements like "Jesus raised Lazarus from the dead." Ulrich Zwingli, the father of many of today's Reformed churches, also claimed that it was only according to his human nature that Christ suffered and died and the "communion of idioms" was at best only a figure of speech. He believed it was more reverent and fitting to speak of the man Jesus as the subject of all human activities and of God (the Logos) as the only subject of divine activity.

In current, scholarly discussions too, a major disconnection between the human and divine natures of Christ has occurred. Many contemporary scholars divide the "man Jesus" from the "Christ of faith." Through "historical studies" that adopt a critical view of the Scriptures, these scholars try to discover their own version of the "human Christ." "Jesus Seminar" scholars have voted to decide on which sayings of Jesus are authentic and which are not;

most, they have decided for us, are not. Meanwhile, such contemporary theology teaches that the Christ of faith, in whom the church believes as divine, can only be "experienced in community with other Christians of the same tradition." In all such thinking and teaching, the "human" and "divine" Christs, if either really exists, are kept strictly separate from each other.

The redemptive value of our salvation, however, rests on the truth that God's own eternal Son was born of a woman, took on our nature, became our substitute, lived a perfect life, and died an innocent death in order to set us free from sin. The Bible ascribes to the entire person of Christ both divine and human qualities. At the same time, it reminds us that the two natures each contribute particular characteristics to that divine-human person. So Christ is eternal yet existed in time. He possesses both divine and human characteristics, each according to its own nature, not commingled but united in the God-man. And we repeat once more: this is a mystery beyond all of our human powers to comprehend. In Christ, God became one of us. From the time of his incarnation through all eternity, he is true God and true man in one divine-human person and possesses fully all the qualities and characteristics of both natures.

The majestic genus

The second class of Bible passages having to do with the communion of properties is called the majestic genus. Passages that fall into this grouping teach that the Son of God, by virtue of the personal union, communicates to his human nature, for common possession, all the properties of his divine nature. When Christ, who possessed the divine nature from eternity, took on a human nature, the divine nature assumed the human into itself without robbing it of its identity. Since the human nature has been assumed into the divine, it shares in the entire glory and majesty of that nature, as well as in all its divine properties and characteristics. With the apostle Paul the church has always joyously confessed that "in Christ all the fullness of the Deity lives in bodily form" (Colossians 2:9).

Note carefully how the apostle piles one term upon another in his key verse. All the fullness of God means all the qualities and characteristics of the divine being, everything that makes him God. All that is fundamentally a quality of the second person of the eternal God-being assumed permanent habitation in the human body and soul of Jesus. The more we probe this statement, the less we understand, and the more we adore. Jesus' human nature, because it is united in one person with the divine nature of the second person of the eternal Trinity, has permanently received and continually shares in the divine power, knowledge, and glory of God.

The Bible speaks in particular of Christ's human nature sharing in the divine characteristics of omnipotence (John 13:3), omniscience (John 2:24,25), omnipresence (Ephesians 4:10), and divine honor and glory (John 5:23; Philippians 2:9-11). The Spirit was given to Jesus' human nature without measure (John 3:34). Since the Spirit is the Spirit of wisdom and knowledge, Christ, also according to his human nature, received infinite divine wisdom and knowledge. Even in his state of humiliation, Jesus possessed the almighty powers that enabled him to heal the sick, cast out demons, and perform other miracles.

"What kind of man is this?" the disciples asked in wonder after Jesus had stilled the storm (Matthew 8:27).

"Even the winds and the waves obey him!" The property of divine power had been communicated to Jesus' human nature. By virtue of his human nature, Jesus was locally and visibly present with his disciples. But because divine omnipresence was communicated to that nature, Jesus could also comfort his disciples with the assurance, "And surely I am with you always, to the very end of the age" (Matthew 28:20).

When Christians worship Jesus, they worship the God-man according to both his human and divine natures. Since the divine nature communicated its attributes to the human nature, we ascribe divine properties to both natures of Christ. To the divine nature we ascribe them essentially, because they inherently belong to that nature. To the human nature we ascribe them by way of communication, as "all the fullness of the Deity" living "in bodily form" (Colossians 2:9).

Again on the basis of human reason, ancient and modern teachers in the tradition of Zwingli and others refuse to acknowledge the majestic genus. They teach that it is impossible for Christ's human nature to share in the divine qualities. The finite, they argue, is not capable of containing the infinite. According to this view, Christ's human nature would be destroyed if the properties of the divine nature were thrust upon it. So their claim is that in the uniting of the two natures, the human nature of Jesus received great power, knowledge, and wisdom, but not full divine knowledge, power, and wisdom. It was also that kind of thinking that led Zwingli to teach that Jesus' body, since his ascension, is locally circumscribed in heaven. A human body can only be in one place at a time, Zwingli argued. Therefore, it is impossible for Jesus to continually give his body and blood to believers on earth to eat and to drink in diverse times and in each succeeding age.

Scripture, however, clearly affirms that the human nature of Christ did indeed receive divine omnipotence, authority to execute judgment, divine omniscience, omnipresence, and all the other properties the divine nature has possessed from eternity.

In John 1:14, the apostle John expressly states, "We have seen his glory." The divine glory given to Christ's human nature was evident to those around him even in the days of his humiliation. According to his divine nature, Jesus has possessed everything from all eternity. The divine properties he displayed in time were also shared with his assumed human nature. To remove all doubt from the disciples' minds on this point, Jesus permitted three of them, including John, to be eyewitnesses of his divine majesty as he allowed it to shine from, with, and through his human nature during his transfiguration (Luke 9:28-36). And the passage in Colossians chapter 2, which we quoted previously, assures us that all the fullness of the Deity dwells in the human Christ. The man Jesus—who was crucified, died, and was buried—is true God. He came, the apostle John tells us in 1 John 5:6, "by water and blood . . . [not] by water only, but by water and blood." The Spirit of God didn't descend on Jesus at his baptism and then withdraw from him before his death, as Paul of Samosata and various others who have taken up his false teachings have claimed, but Jesus was God both when he was baptized in the Jordan and when he was crucified on Calvary's cross. The majesty of God was shared by his human nature without essentially altering that nature. Jesus' human nature was a fit organ for the eternal Word. All who looked at the face of Christ looked at the face of God.

This communication of divine properties to Jesus' human nature is, of course, not reciprocal. The human nature cannot add or contribute anything to the divine nature. But by virtue of the personal union, the human nature shares in all the divine properties by communication. During Jesus' state of humiliation, not all of these properties were fully and completely used. In his state of exaltation they are.

The apotelesmatic genus

The third category of the communion of properties is known as the apotelesmatic genus. This group of Scripture references shows that in all Christ's official acts as our Redeemer (apotelesms), both in his humiliation and exaltation, each nature performed what is peculiar to itself but always with the full participation of the other. Scripture passages that describe apotelesms include those which describe Christ's official function with names such as Savior, Mediator, Prophet, High Priest, and King. They also include passages that describe his official acts as our Savior: bearing our sins, dying for our sins, offering himself as a sacrifice to God, destroying the devil's work. An example of apotelesms is Luke 2:11: "Today in the town of David a Savior has been born to you; he is Christ the Lord." To be born is a property of human nature. To be Savior and Lord is a property of the divine nature. Both natures participated fully in Christ's birth. Also 1 John 3:8 reads, "The reason the Son of God appeared was to destroy the devil's work." Son of God is a divine name and includes all the divine properties. To "appear" is a property of human nature. Both natures participated in the Savior's incarnation, each nature performing what was peculiar to itself. And with both natures fully participating, Jesus met and defeated Satan and destroyed the destroyer and his work. Both natures of Christ fully participated in all of his acts of redemption (apotelesms), each nature performing what is peculiar to itself, yet as one undivided Christ.

All of this is eternally important for us. Christ's redemptive work could be accomplished only because in him the divine and human natures were united as they are. By itself, in the abstract, the divine nature cannot suffer or die. By itself, in the abstract, the human nature could not be a universal substitute for the human race. But the God-man could and did suffer and die to fulfill God's redemptive plan for mankind's salvation, to satisfy divine justice, and to earn forgiveness of sins, a restored relationship with God, and eternal life for the whole world of sinners. The divine nature did not itself die but participated in the act of dying through its union with the human nature. By communicating its properties to the human nature, the divine nature strengthened and sustained that nature as the God-man fulfilled God's eternal plan of redemption perfectly, fully, and completely through his suffering and death.

Whether the Savior is described according to either or both natures, the works of his office are always performed by his entire person with both natures involved. From this union his work receives its completeness and success. For this purpose the Son of God assumed a human nature. As we study his humiliation and exaltation, his office, and his work, we do not see two natures, one working separately or acting out its part independently without the participation of the other. Rather, we see one divine-human Christ, the two natures wondrously and mysteriously united in perfect communion, each contributing what is particular to itself with the full participation of the other, together sufficient to fulfill God's eternal plan to save us.

The primary proclamation of the Christian church will always be the forgiveness of sins purchased by Christ and the righteousness of Christ given as a free gift to sinners by God's grace. Believers will rest their hope simply, always, and alone in the whole Christ of the gospels, the one who has no beginning or end yet entered the world of time as one of us and walked the dusty roads of Palestine from dawn to dusk. He made all things yet grew thirsty and tired. He lives in eternal bliss yet experienced the horror of death and hell; he is the one who is pure, sweet goodness yet experienced temptation and fought real battles with the evil one. He as our brother lived, died, and rose again, was exalted to the heavenly realms, and now rules all things with his power, even as he intercedes for us. As our brother, he is present with us now. As our brother, he is living out his life in us now; as our brother, he is bringing us to glory now and will one day bring us home. He is the God-man. In this man we find God. He is the God-man, our kinsman and Redeemer, the one we worship and adore.

6

Applying the Doctrine of the Two Natures of Christ

The teaching that Jesus Christ is both God and man in one person is one of Christianity's most vital and fundamental truths. Any study of Jesus Christ our Savior must of necessity include a thorough study of his person. In this first rather lengthy section of this volume, we have done that. In the course of these chapters, there have been unfamiliar terms and difficult concepts. There have also been some overlapping and repetition as we learned of Christ's divine and human natures and their relationship to each other. But as we bring this section to a close, we need to be reminded too that, like all of Scripture's teachings, the teaching concerning Jesus' person is not just a matter of facts we learn as an intellectual exercise. This is a teaching that speaks to and stimulates faith. And it has important applications, both for our salvation and for our daily lives.

That the Creator took on our human nature and became a creature, that the eternal Son of God became a man, "equal to the Father as to his deity, less than the Father as to his humanity,"[23] is a marvelous mystery. And it is absolutely vital to our salvation. Our salvation, Luther once remarked, depends as much on Christ's human nature as on his deity. Colossians 1:20 tells us that it was God's will to reconcile all things to himself through Christ "by making peace through his blood, shed on the cross." God's plan for man's salvation called for a perfect substitute and the shedding of blood. That made it necessary for Jesus to become true man. We should not, however, view the taking on of the human nature by the second person of the eternal Trinity in itself as an act of humiliation on Christ's part. If his humiliation consisted in his becoming human, then his exaltation would have had to consist in the putting off of the human nature. But we do not read of the "excarnation" of Christ. Christ's humiliation consisted both in the lowly manner of his incarnation and the fact that, during the time he carried out his substitutionary, redemptive work for mankind, he laid aside the full and constant use of his divine power and majesty. He could have come into the world trailing clouds of glory. But he didn't. Instead, he assumed the lowly form of a servant. He became subject to the limitations and weaknesses of human nature. He placed himself under the law as the substitute for the human race. And so, as Paul powerfully writes in Philippians 2:8, "He humbled himself and became obedient to death—even death on a cross!"

The first and most important application of the doctrine of Jesus' person, therefore, is its necessity for our salvation (Hebrews 2:17). If Christ had not been true God from all eternity, he could never have met God's requirements, completed God's plan, and accomplished our salvation. If Christ had not taken on our human nature, he could not have suffered in our place or been our substitute in any way. Martin Luther never tired of emphasizing that truth:

> The most precious treasure and the strongest consolation we Christians have is this: that the Word, the true and natural Son of God, became man, with flesh and blood like that of any other human; that He became incarnate for our sakes in order that we might enter into great glory, that our flesh and blood, skin and hair, hands and feet, stomach and back might reside in heaven as God does.[24]

But there's also another application of the truth that Jesus is true man that we should not overlook, because of the comfort that it brings. By taking on a human nature, Jesus became our brother (Hebrews 2:11). He became one of us in every respect, but without sin. That means that Jesus understands us, not just because he is true God and understands everything but also because he felt what we feel and experienced what we experience. When we experience pain, he understands because he experienced it too. He too grew tired and weary (John 4:6). He too experienced the grief we experience when a loved one is taken from us by death (John 11:33-35). He was forsaken by friends, even betrayed by one of them (Matthew 26:48,49). He was rejected by the very people he came to help. He also knows what it means to be tempted, for he was tempted too (Hebrews 2:18). What encouragement it brings us to know that he knows, that he sympathizes, that he cares, that he understands! Perhaps the writer to the Hebrews put it best when he declared, "We do not have a high priest who is unable to sympathize with our weaknesses, but we have one who has been tempted in every way, just as we are—yet was without sin" (4:15).

Similarly, the truth that Jesus is true God has important applications for both our salvation and our daily lives. The Bible tells us, "The blood of Jesus, his Son, purifies us from all sin" (1 John 1:7). If Jesus' blood had been the blood of a mere man, it could not have purified himself, much less anyone else. But because it is the blood of him who is true God, it has atoning power and infinite value. We are saved from the punishment of hell that we deserve, because the atoning blood of Jesus is the blood of God. "The person [of Jesus]," Luther wrote, "is eternal and infinite, and even one little drop of his blood would have been enough to save the entire world."[25]

There is also rich and precious comfort in knowing that the very Savior who loved us so much that he gave his life to save us is true God. Now highly exalted, he rules over all things in heaven and on earth. He who as the God-man experienced all that we experience, who sympathizes with us in our weakness and understands all our troubles by virtue of his own experience, rules the world and all things for the welfare of his believers and in the interest of his church. Nothing can harm us since we are the objects of his unfailing love.

Yes, the doctrine of the person of Christ is important. It is one of those key truths on which our salvation rests. That alone makes it practical and applicable. It gives authority to everything he says. But what comfort and encouragement the teaching concerning Christ's person also brings as it assures us each day that the God-man is our Savior, our Comforter, our Shepherd, our brother, and our friend.

Part II

THE HUMILIATION AND

EXALTATION OF CHRIST

7

The "Beggar's Cloak"

From the very moment of his conception, Jesus' divine and human natures were inseparably united in one divine-human person, one God-man. No observant reader of the gospels, however, can fail to conclude that during the time that Jesus, the God-man, lived and worked on earth, there were two very distinct states of his existence. Passages like Isaiah chapter 53 in the Old Testament and Philippians 2:6-11 in the New Testament clearly define two distinct states of existence in the Savior's life. From the time he was conceived by the Holy Spirit up to and including the time of his burial, Jesus lived as a man among men. The majestic glory that his human nature possessed by virtue of its union with the divine nature, though it shined forth at times, for the most part lay hidden under what Luther described as the "beggar's cloak" of his human nature. We call this state of his existence Jesus' *state of humiliation*. After his defeat of death and the grave, however, particularly after he appeared alive again after his resurrection, Jesus' state of existence differed from what it had been before. No longer was his divine glory hidden. His disciples and all who observed him constantly saw him display and use his full divine majesty and glory in his *state of exaltation*. That state of exaltation continues today as Jesus rules the universe with his almighty power. And we await his return in glory as judge of all the earth.

The incarnation of Christ consisted essentially in the miracle that the Son of God, who possessed all the fullness of the divine nature, took on a true human nature. He entered a unique personal union with a nature like our own. From the very moment of the incarnation, the human nature shared in the full possession of all the divine characteristics, majesty, and glory. However, as an essential element of his redemptive work for us, Jesus, from the time of his conception to the time he was made alive again after his burial, took on what Saint Paul describes in Philippians 2:7 as "the very nature of a servant."

In that state of existence, Jesus experienced all the weaknesses of human nature after the fall, though not the sin. He voluntarily placed himself under the divine law, though he himself is Lord of all. And he bore the curse of the law as the substitutionary sacrifice for the sins of all mankind. This condition, this self-renunciation, is referred to as Christ's state of humiliation. We define this state as the time during which Christ voluntarily renounced the full use of his divine powers and the full exercise of his divine majesty, that he might place himself under God's law as man's substitute and suffer and die to redeem the world.

Jesus' state of humiliation was made possible by his incarnation. The divine nature cannot change; therefore, it cannot be humbled or exalted. And the incarnation was itself a marvelous act of condescension on the part of the second person of the eternal Trinity, hence a part of the humiliation. But the incarnation and Jesus' humiliation must not be regarded as one and the same thing. The state of humiliation began with the incarnation. And it came to an end when Jesus' exaltation began. The fact that Jesus became the God-man had a beginning. But it has no end. The incarnate Jesus is now the exalted God-man, who lives and rules eternally.

Jesus remained true God

The Bible also makes it clear that though Jesus endured humiliation, his humiliation did not change the essential nature of Christ. He is and will ever remain God. Even in the days of his humiliation, the Bible ascribes to Jesus full possession of all the divine majesty and every divine quality and characteristic. By entering a state of humiliation, Jesus didn't give away his divine nature. He never stopped being true God as well as true man. But in a marvelous act that goes beyond our human ability to explain, he laid aside the full and constant use of his divine prerogatives and characteristics according to his human nature. Thus the Bible speaks of a Christ who possessed all riches, yet owned nothing; a Christ who knows all things, yet was limited in knowledge. The Bible speaks of a Christ who is Creator and Lord of all, yet was subject to sinful human beings; a Christ who is the Prince of life, yet died a real death on Calvary's cross.

Such utterly opposing statements could never be made about any human being. But all are true of Jesus. The Bible teaches that in the days of his flesh, during the years he lived in his state of humiliation, Jesus did not always use what was his to use as the God-man. The Lutheran Confessions use words like *concealed* and *restrained* to describe this phenomenon.[26] The divine nature and its attendant characteristics, including almighty power, were always there. The full weight of Jesus' divinity, attached to his substitutionary work, gave it infinite value. But in his humiliation, according to his human nature, Jesus didn't always use the wealth of the divine power at his disposal. He suffered because he allowed himself to suffer. And he died because he did not use his power to live.

Jesus humbled himself willingly and voluntarily so that he could carry out the work of redemption through a substitutionary sacrifice. Had he always used the divine majesty that was his, as he did at his transfiguration and after his resurrection, he could not have been our substitute. He could not have rendered perfect obedience and died in our place.

The fact that Jesus' state of humiliation corresponds to the days of his life and ministry on earth doesn't mean that during that time Jesus never used his divine glory or displayed his divine characteristics at all. We have already mentioned the transfiguration. Jesus performed miracles. He carried out a prophetic ministry and acted as our perfect High Priest. And not only was his human nature sustained by the divine power imparted to it in the agony of his passion, but even then the rays of his divine glory shone forth through the gloom. A cursory reading of the passion history is enough to reveal countless evidences of

Jesus' divinity. Think, for example, of how he healed the man whom Peter had wounded in the garden (Luke 22:51) and knocked those who had come to capture him to the ground with a single word (John 18:4-6). The entire passion history was orchestrated, timed, and directed not by Jesus' enemies, as they supposed, but by Jesus himself (Matthew 26:18). The time had come for him to bring his work as our substitute and Savior to its climax. And he would not be deterred from that work. The use or nonuse of his divine majesty was governed by Christ's office as our Redeemer. Because he humbled himself by refraining from the full and constant use of his divine majesty and rendered perfect obedience to the Father, Jesus fulfilled his office as our Redeemer. His poverty is our riches (2 Corinthians 8:9); his blood is our righteousness; his death is our eternal ransom.

When the Bible teaches that Jesus humbled himself and "made himself nothing" (Philippians 2:7), it does not teach that he ceased to be God. Nor does it teach that he divested himself of his omniscience, omnipotence, omnipresence, or any of the other divine qualities that he possessed from eternity. The false teaching that claims he did is called *kenoticism*, from a Greek word meaning "empty." Kenoticism is yet another false teaching concerning Jesus' person promoted by some Reformed teachers and their followers. According to those who teach a "kenosis," Jesus' divine nature was reduced or diminished by his incarnation. Kenoticism, however, contradicts all the Scripture passages which tell us that even in his humiliation, Jesus continued to be one with the Father in essence. The Bible teaches that Jesus' divine mode of existence was not changed by his incarnation (John 10:30). Nor was his divine mode of activity (John 5:17,19). Kenoticism makes the mistake of transforming the unchangeable God into a being subject to change.

When the Bible teaches that Jesus humbled himself, it doesn't teach that Jesus gave up his divine qualities or allowed his divinity to be diminished in any way. What it does teach is that he set aside the full and continuous use of those qualities. Jesus, during the days of his humiliation, didn't always or fully use the divine majesty imparted by his divine nature to his human nature. He humbled himself willingly and voluntarily so that he could complete the work the Father had given him to do and serve as our Redeemer.

Philippians 2:6-11

The classic Scripture passage defining the humiliation—and later also the exaltation—of our Savior is Philippians 2:6-11. In that passage Paul tells us that Jesus' humiliation consists in the fact that during his life on earth the incarnate Son did not appear in the form of God but was found "in appearance as a man." That all the fullness of the Deity lived in him (Colossians 2:9) is unquestioned. Jesus possessed all the divine majesty; all the divine properties were communicated to his human nature. But Jesus didn't always and fully show the majesty he possessed. He didn't come to earth to flaunt his divinity or to impress people with his mighty acts. But he appeared in the form of a servant. He covered his majesty with that "beggar's cloak" of his human nature. He led the life of an ordinary human being, experiencing all of human life. Nor did that human nature disappear after his exaltation, for the Bible speaks of him now as the eternally exalted God-man.

Paul's powerful words in Philippians chapter 2 cannot possibly mean anything else than that Christ, in humbling himself according to his human nature, refrained from the full and constant use of the divine majesty imparted to that nature at the incarnation. To serve us and to save us, Christ could not have laid aside his divinity. The full weight of his deity had to be attached to his obedience, suffering, and death to give it value. He had to meet and defeat death and rise again, conquering death by dying. To do that he had to lay aside for a time the full use of the majesty of God according to his human nature. So Christ "emptied himself," not by giving up his divine prerogatives or characteristics but by giving up their full and constant use. And, obedient to the Father's plan, he suffered the ultimate depths of physical and spiritual humiliation, together with the eternal separation from God that accompanied it. Human language struggles to give adequate expression to what Jesus did. The Lord's apostle says it best in this passage from Philippians: "And being found in appearance as a man, he humbled himself and became obedient to death—even death on a cross!" (verse 8).

The history of Christ's humiliation

The history of Christ's humiliation included all the events of his earthly life. That history is often summarized in these words of the Apostles' Creed: "[He] was conceived by the Holy Spirit, born of the virgin Mary, suffered under Pontius Pilate, was crucified, died, and was buried."

Conception and birth

Jesus' conception and birth were a part of his humiliation. His incarnation, his taking on of his human nature, was not in itself humiliation but a mighty miracle. The manner, however, in which the Son of God took on a human nature was humiliation. Jesus did not enter the world with all the pomp and glory that was fitting for a heavenly king. But he was conceived in a virgin's womb, born as a helpless infant, and laid in a lowly manger. He who is true God from eternity became dependent on a human mother for his physical care. And by his incarnation, God's Son, though he did not take on human sin, took on all the weakness, frailty, and limitations that are now common to human beings as general consequences of sin in a sinful world. The almighty Lord of the universe became subject to the laws of time and space. Though not specifically mentioned in the words of the Apostles' Creed, Jesus' circumcision, education, and the whole of his earthly life and ministry were all included in his humiliation. As all Jewish male infants were circumcised on the eighth day, Jesus, as part of his voluntary subjection to divine law, was circumcised (Luke 2:21). Though he had no sin, no faults that required correction by education, he nevertheless, by real study, increased in wisdom according to his human nature (Luke 2:52). In his state of humiliation, he did not always fully use the divine omniscience that was his as the God-man (Matthew 24:36). In his visible sojourn on earth, Jesus truly appeared in the form of a servant.

Public ministry

In his servant's form of humiliation, Jesus began his public ministry with a 40-day struggle with Satan in the wilderness (Matthew 4:1-11). The evangelists tell us that the devil tried to exploit the fact that Jesus was hungry, a human limitation that he took on as part of his humiliation. Nor did Jesus yield to the devil's temptation to use the divine power he possessed in a way that was inappropriate or contrary to the Father's will. The fact that he who is true

God as well as true man was tempted at all was part of his humiliation. The fact that he was "tempted in every way, just as we are—yet was without sin" (Hebrews 4:15) was part of his active obedience for us and his success for us where our first parents had failed. In his humiliation, Jesus, though ruler of all, submitted to civil government (Matthew 22:21). He endured the troubles, dangers, and hardships and experienced the emotions that are common to human beings in general. He voluntarily performed the lowliest of tasks, including the washing of his disciples' feet on Maundy Thursday (John 13:5). He lived in a simple and unpretentious way and was regarded as equal or even inferior to those around him (Mark 6:2,3).

Suffering, death, and burial

The climactic events of Jesus' state of humiliation were his suffering, death, and burial. Though Jesus suffered much during his earthly life, his suffering culminated in his great passion during the two days we know as Maundy Thursday and Good Friday. The passion includes the extreme anguish of body and soul that Jesus endured as he went from the upper room to Gethsemane and finally to Golgotha in order to satisfy the Father's divine justice and offer the atoning sacrifice that paid for our sins. Jesus' anguish of soul in Gethsemane; his enduring the travesty of justice in the religious court of the Jews and the civil court of the Gentiles; the false witnesses, scourging, mistreatment, mocking, and finally the shameful slave's death, to which Paul refers with the deliberate and striking phrase "even death on a cross!" (Philippians 2:8), all combined to constitute the depths of his humiliation.

The greatest depths of Jesus' humiliation, however, didn't come with the physical torments of the cross. On

Calvary, Jesus suffered infinitely more than the agony that accompanied this barbaric form of execution. On Calvary, Jesus, in his sinless soul, suffered separation from God (Matthew 27:46). He suffered the very pangs of hell, as God charged to him and he willingly accepted the punishment divine justice demanded for every sin ever committed by human beings. Because he is God, Christ's being forsaken by God for a time was sufficient to ransom all mankind from sin. Because he was willing to humble himself, the debt could be paid. Jesus bore all of those torments without sin, persisting in perfect obedience to and complete trust in his heavenly Father.

"He died and was buried." Jesus' death was a true death, the separation of his soul from his body. But by virtue of the communion of his two natures, his death availed as the sacrifice sufficient to atone for the sins of all people. When Jesus died on Calvary, God died. He did what was contrary to his divine nature. The fact that Jesus could and did humble himself to the depths of death is a mystery beyond our human ability to fathom. He himself describes his willingness to undergo that humiliation in John 10:17,18: "The reason my Father loves me is that I lay down my life—only to take it up again. No one takes it from me, but I lay it down of my own accord."

Jesus died the death he did by laying aside the full use of his divine characteristics and the divine power imparted to his human nature. That the Savior continued to possess those divine qualities, even in the darkest hours of his humiliation, has already been shown. The history of the Savior's passion is the account of how "for us and for our salvation" Jesus went forward to meet the deepest humiliation and the death of the cross to fulfill his mission on earth and to fulfill the prophetic Scriptures. The depths of his humiliation were not forced on him by human power or even Satan's will. He willingly went forward to meet it all, to carry out the Father's will and the saving plan determined from all eternity in the counsels of the triune God.

Jesus' burial, or entombment, constituted the final stage of his humiliation. Jesus' burial was the visible evidence of the reality of his death and brought closure to the events of Calvary. The honorable burial that he received and the preservation without decay of his lifeless body in the grave are presented by both Old and New Testament Scriptures as a special privilege accorded by God to the Messiah, in preparation for his exaltation (Psalm 16:9,10; Isaiah 53:9; Matthew 27:57-60; Acts 2:31; 13:37).

8

Return to Power and Glory

As soon as the humiliation of Christ had accomplished its purpose, his exaltation began. Christ's humiliation consisted in his not fully and not at all times displaying and using the divine majesty he possesses as the God-man. It follows, therefore, that in his exaltation, Jesus, also according to his human nature, now freely and constantly displays and exercises all the prerogatives and qualities of the divine nature he has possessed from all eternity.

Strictly speaking, of course, the humiliation and exaltation have to do only with Jesus' human nature, as the divine nature does not and cannot change. Yet, by virtue of the personal union, we speak of the humiliation and exaltation of the God-man. We can describe Jesus' state of exaltation both negatively and positively. Negatively, it is the permanent putting off of the servant's form, the beggar's cloak that covered his divine glory during much of his life here on earth. Positively, the exaltation can be described as Jesus' entrance into the unrestricted use of his divine glory, which will never cease.

The purpose of the exaltation is not to give Jesus a well-deserved reward for his completed work. Jesus did his work for us, not for himself. But his exaltation follows naturally, as the result of his completed work. During the days of his humiliation, many refused to recognize Jesus as the Lord of glory. Many today regard him only as a human being. But if that exalted Savior were to appear now, as he surely will on the day of judgment, every knee would bow to him and every tongue would have to confess him as Lord and God.

The state of exaltation is not only a state of honor and glory. It is also a state of power and dominion. Philippians 2:9 tells us that having exalted him, God "gave him the name that is above every name." And Ephesians 1:20-22 tells us that with his exaltation, God placed everything under his feet. Jesus' exaltation means that as the God-man, Jesus, also according to his human nature, is now and forever present everywhere. He rules and governs all things as King of kings and Lord of lords. Christ's state of exaltation began with his return to life in the grave. It exhibited itself in the spirit world by his descent into hell. It became visible in our world by his glorious resurrection. And it continues in the highest heavens by his ascension into heaven and his sitting at the right hand of God.

The descent into hell

Early on Easter morning Jesus' soul returned to his body. He who had died on Calvary's cross became alive again.

Immediately after his quickening, he descended into hell. Two New Testament passages, 1 Peter 3:18-20 and Colossians 2:15, describe Christ's descent into hell. Both make it clear that this event was not part of Christ's humiliation but of his exaltation. Peter tells us, "He was put to death in the body but made alive by the Spirit, through whom also he went and preached to the spirits in prison" (verses 18,19). The phrase "in the body" corresponds to Jesus' state of humiliation. "By the Spirit" denotes that new life in exaltation which began when he became alive again and never ends.[27] Having been made alive, Jesus descended into hell. He descended not only in his divine nature or as a disembodied spirit but as the living and exalted God-man.

In hell, Christ made a proclamation to the demons and to the damned. We note that Christ didn't descend into hell to suffer. His suffering was complete when from the cross he cried out, "It is finished." Jesus didn't descend into hell to pay a ransom to the devil. Nor did he enter hell to rescue the souls of those who were trapped there or to give them another opportunity to heed the gospel and repent. Hebrews 9:27 teaches that "man is destined to die once, and after that to face judgment." But Jesus entered the realm of the demons and the damned to proclaim his victory. Like a conqueror in a war, who goes directly to the capital of the enemies he has defeated and demands unconditional surrender, Jesus descended into hell and "made a public spectacle" of his enemies, "triumphing over them by the cross" (Colossians 2:15). By his descent into hell, Jesus revealed himself to his enemies as victor over sin and Satan, death and hell. We aren't told how Jesus' proclamation to the demons and the damned was made. But the mere fact that he showed himself alive to those suffering in hell was enough to convince hell's residents that Jesus is Lord and their judgment is just.

The doctrine of Christ's descent into hell is also a comfort to believers. It assures us that because Christ paid for all our sins on the cross, Satan has lost his claim on mankind. He can no longer accuse us before God. He can no longer control our lives because his power has been broken. Christ is the victor. And through the gospel, Christ shares the fruits of his victory with us.

The resurrection

The most significant event in Christ's exaltation is his resurrection from the dead. Jesus rose to give evidence to all the world that he had won the victory as mankind's perfect substitute. Because Jesus is God, it was impossible for death to hold him. And because death could not hold Jesus, believers have spiritual and eternal life in him.

There were no eyewitnesses of Jesus' resurrection. The angel rolled the stone away from the tomb not to let Jesus escape but to reveal to all the world that the tomb was empty and that Jesus had risen. Despite the fact that there were no eyewitnesses to the resurrection event itself, the resurrection of Jesus is the most carefully documented event in all of Scripture. The gospel writers, as well as the apostle Paul, list witness upon witness who saw the risen Christ. The resurrection of Jesus is a documented historical fact that cannot be disproved. As such it stands as a fundamental article of the Christian faith.

Precisely because the resurrection of Jesus is so vital to the Christian faith, the enemies of Christianity, both ancient and modern, have directed some of their heaviest attacks at Scripture's resurrection accounts. Already on Easter morning, Jesus' Jewish enemies bribed the Roman soldiers to say that Jesus hadn't risen from the dead at all. They were to say that the disciples had stolen his body and claimed he had risen (Matthew 28:12-15). This *theft* theory is still spooking around among unbelievers today. The *swoon* theory is the idea that Jesus never really died but was only in a near-death state when his body was removed from the cross. He later regained consciousness, left the tomb, and convinced the disciples that he had risen. Muslims, among others, teach that Jesus never really died and that Simon of Cyrene, or even Judas Iscariot, took his place on the cross. The *hallucination* theory holds that the disciples thought they saw things they really didn't.

Many modern scholars subscribe to a kind of *pious fraud* theory, which suggests that the resurrection was something the disciples made up later as a symbol conferring saving significance on the cross. Rudolf Bultmann, the twentieth-century German theologian who had a great influence on modern theology, went so far as to call the resurrection a myth borrowed from the thought-world of the first century, with its stories of dying and rising gods. The early disciples, he reasoned, proclaimed that Jesus was alive in order to express his special, exalted relationship with God. To such modern scholars, the resurrection of Jesus is not history but part of the proclamation of the church. And believing in the resurrection in this way is simply another way of saying that Jesus is the Christ—whatever that happens to mean to you.

For every one of these denials that the resurrection took place there are compelling counterarguments. It is highly unlikely that 11 terrified men who were still hiding behind locked doors on Easter evening would have even attempted to steal Jesus' body from the heavily guarded tomb. It is even more unlikely that they could have succeeded. Jesus' death on the cross wasn't just apparent. It was real. John witnessed the piercing of Jesus' side and reported in the third person, "The man who saw it [John himself] has given testimony, and his testimony is true. He knows that he tells the truth, and he testifies so that you also may believe" (John 19:35). Jesus' postresurrection appearances to his disciples were so frequent and his activity so open that a hallucination theory is nothing short of ludicrous. If Jesus' tomb had not been empty, as the apostles declared it to be on Pentecost (Acts 2:29-36) and afterward, their testimony of the risen Christ could easily have been disproved. But it wasn't. Nor would those first disciples have risked persecution, prison, and even death to proclaim a story they had invented and to perpetrate a fraud they knew wasn't true. Every unbelieving argument against Jesus' resurrection fails, and we are left with this wondrous truth: "He is risen indeed."

That the historicity of Jesus' resurrection is challenged by modern skeptics and opponents of Christianity shouldn't surprise us. Just verses after he recorded the awesome event of the resurrection itself, Matthew recorded the Jews' attempts to deny it (Matthew 28:12-15). Paul too addressed the question of the historic fact of the resurrection. Some of the educated Corinthians, it appears, wondered about whether the dead could rise. If the dead don't rise, Paul argued in 1 Corinthians chapter 15, Christ could not have risen. And if Christ has not risen, Christian preaching is futile and Christian faith is worthless (verses 12-14).

In all of his epistles, including the earliest epistles he wrote, 1 and 2 Thessalonians and Galatians, Paul speaks confidently about Jesus' resurrection. In 1 Corinthians chapter 15, known as the apostle's great resurrection chapter, Paul cites a host of eyewitnesses of the resurrection. They include the Eleven; five hundred disciples to whom the risen Christ appeared at once; James, an early leader of the Jerusalem church; and himself, to whom the risen Christ, after his ascension, appeared in a vision near Damascus. Paul proclaimed what the church from its inception had proclaimed, the gospel of a Christ who died, was buried, and rose again. The earliest creeds place Jesus' death and resurrection side by side. If the first is true, the second must follow if Jesus is truly the God-man, the Christ.

The significance of Jesus' resurrection

There are many reasons why Jesus' resurrection is the key event in his exaltation and is vital to our Christian faith. Not only Jesus' suffering and death but also his resurrection fulfilled the Old Testament Scriptures (Acts 2:25-31). Careful readers of the New Testament will observe that Jesus himself always followed his own prophecies of his death with clear promises of his resurrection (Matthew 16:21). He proclaimed himself as the one who had the divine authority both to lay down his life and to take it up again (John 10:18). The careful documentation of the resurrection in both the gospels and the epistles assures us that the resurrection of Jesus is not some new article of faith. It is an integral part of Jesus' own proclamation about himself. It is an essential element in all that "the Law of Moses, the Prophets and the Psalms" testified about the coming Messiah (Luke 24:44).

Jesus' resurrection proves beyond all doubt that he is God and his message is the truth. The miracles that Jesus performed during his earthly ministry were certainly sufficient to establish that truth. But the Jews refused to believe the miracles. They kept demanding more signs. Finally, Jesus promised them the "sign of the prophet Jonah" (Matthew 12:39). This was a reference to the fact that as Jonah was in the belly of the great fish for three days and was then set free, so after three days in the grave Jesus would rise again. Because Jesus did rise, Paul could conclude, "[He] was declared with power to be the Son of God by his resurrection from the dead" (Romans 1:4). If Jesus is indeed the Son of God, his teachings are completely true. Jesus had to be either the Son of God or a deceiving fraud. There are no other possibilities. Had he been a deceiver or a fraud, he could never have risen from the dead. But he did rise. He was seen by many witnesses. By the resurrection, the Father declared once more that Jesus is his beloved Son and Jesus' teachings are divinely true.

Jesus' resurrection is the guarantee that his work is complete and that God has declared the whole world justified and forgiven in Christ. If Christ had remained dead and buried in the tomb, it would have been clear evidence that his suffering and death had not been sufficient to atone for sins or to reconcile the world to the holy God (1 Corinthians 15:17). But the fact that Jesus did rise is conclusive evidence that the Father has accepted the Son's sacrifice. "He [Jesus] was delivered over to death for our sins," Paul writes in Romans 4:25, "and was raised to life for our justification." By raising Christ from the dead, the Father declared that sufficient payment had been made for the sins of all mankind. Christ took the sins of every human being with him to the cross, where he voluntarily endured the punishment that divine justice demanded for them all. His resurrection proves that the payment is complete and the world is reconciled to God. In God's "great exchange," the world's sins were charged to Christ and Christ's righteousness credited to the sinful world (2 Corinthians 5:21). The resurrection is God's formal declaration of mankind's absolution, the declaration that Christ has purchased forgiveness and new life for all.

Finally, Jesus' resurrection proves that there is such a thing as a resurrection from the dead. The risen Christ is the "firstfruits of those who have fallen asleep" (1 Corinthians 15:20). His resurrection guarantees his promise that on the day of his return in glory, he will raise our bodies, which will be separated from our souls at physical death. He will give our bodies life again, glorify them by clothing them with sinless perfection, and reunite them with our souls. Following that great day, all believers, in both body and soul, will spend eternity in glory with the glorified Lord.

The resurrected body of Jesus is the same body that he had assumed in the womb of the virgin Mary and that suffered and died on the cross. But it is now a glorified body, with no limitations. In his exalted state, Christ's body is no longer subject to the laws of time and space, as it was during his humiliation. During the 40 days between his resurrection and his ascension, Christ appeared and disappeared, was recognized or not recognized at will. He ate with his disciples, not because he needed nourishment in his exalted state but simply to prove that he had truly become alive and the disciples weren't seeing a spirit (Luke 24:41-43). In his exaltation, Jesus the God-man, in both his divine and human natures, makes full and complete use of all the qualities and characteristics of God. We can't fully understand or describe what this means because of the limitations of our human minds. But we are assured that in the resurrection life our bodies too will be transformed and changed "so that they will be like his glorious body" (Philippians 3:21). Our resurrected bodies will not have the qualities of God, as the body of Jesus has. But they will be glorified. What an amazing prospect! What a comforting promise!

One other question is sometimes asked in connection with Jesus' resurrection. Is it proper to say that God raised Jesus, or did Jesus raise himself from the dead? In reality, both statements are true. According to the Scriptures, the resurrection was, on one hand, the work of the Father, who by raising Christ declared to the world that Christ's work was successful and complete (Acts 2:24). The Bible also speaks of Christ's raising himself as evidence of his divine nature and almighty power (John 2:19). There is no contradiction here, because Scripture teaches that in all matters pertaining to us and to our salvation, and that would surely include Christ's resurrection, all three persons of the Trinity are at work in perfect harmony.

Although it was certainly the key and central event, Christ's resurrection was not the final event in his exaltation. The Apostles' Creed names three further "steps" in his exaltation. One, his ascension, has already taken place. A second, his sitting at God's right hand, is taking place right now. The third, his return in glory as judge of all the earth, is yet to take place.

The ascension

Jesus' ascension into heaven could be compared to a coronation. Earthly rulers assume all the powers of leadership as soon as they succeed to the throne, generally when a predecessor dies. From that moment on, they are absolute rulers in their kingdoms. The formal acknowledgment of the assumption of rule, however, comes at a stately, prearranged ceremony, a coronation. So Jesus, from the moment he was made alive again on Easter morning, took up again the full and complete use of the divine power and majesty he possessed from all eternity. His resurrection and postresurrection appearances proved that he had entered his exalted state. The ascension formally and publicly acknowledged it.

During the 40 days between his resurrection and ascension, Jesus did not live and work among his disciples in the humble, familiar manner in which he had before. Still, he repeatedly appeared to them. And they acknowledged him as their victorious Lord. Those postresurrection appearances of Jesus provided visible evidence that he had risen. Jesus also used them as opportunities to further instruct the disciples about the saving mission he had now completed. Luke tells us, "He appeared to them over a period of forty days and spoke about the kingdom of God" (Acts 1:3). It was also during those 40 days that Jesus outlined what the disciples' mission and the mission of the New Testament church would be: "You will be my witnesses" (Acts 1:8).

Unlike his resurrection, which no one actually saw take place, Jesus' ascension was visible to his disciples. On the 40th day after he rose from the dead, Jesus took the disciples out to the Mount of Olives near Bethany. There he lifted up his hands to bless them. As he blessed them, he was visibly taken up to heaven before their wondering eyes until a cloud hid him from their sight (Luke 24:50,51; Acts 1:9). Thus Jesus formally and visibly brought an end to his ministry on earth and took up his reign in glory. The fact that Jesus visibly ascended, however, does not mean that he is now confined to a local or circumscribed place. As the eternally exalted God-man, Jesus, in accord with his promises and in both his divine and human natures, is present everywhere, not visibly, but spiritually and invisibly. That omnipresence is a special blessing to his believers, who cherish his parting promise, "Surely I am with you always, to the very end of the age" (Matthew 28:20). Each day believers have their ascended Lord's promise that he is ruling in their hearts. Each day they have the assurance that he is walking beside them as Shepherd and Savior, Guardian and Friend (Matthew 18:20).

The heaven to which Jesus ascended must not be conceived of as limited in any way or as a part of the created, physical world. If that were true, the ascension would have only been a kind of space odyssey in which Jesus was physically transported from one place to another. The Bible, however, describes the ascended Jesus as seated "in the heavenly realms, far above all rule and authority, power and dominion" (Ephesians 1:20,21). Glorified and ascended, his redemptive work complete, Jesus has cast off all the limitations of time and space and lives and reigns with the Father and Spirit in eternal glory. To think of Jesus' existence now as limited in any way, or to speculate, as do the Reformed, that because Jesus ascended into heaven, he cannot be physically present in the Lord's Supper, is to limit that which is unlimited. It is to try to comprehend that which cannot be comprehended by human reason.

Sitting at the right hand of God

Together with Jesus' ascension into heaven goes the truth that he sits at the right hand of the majesty of God. The right hand of God is picture language for the glory and majesty of God. To be at God's right hand means to occupy the position of supreme power and dominion. Christ's sitting at the right hand of God means that he, the exalted

God-man, exercises all the power, rule, and authority of God. He governs the entire universe as King of kings and Lord of lords (Revelation 17:14). This divine majesty has belonged to Jesus from all eternity. It was communicated to his human nature at his incarnation. During his humiliation, he refrained from making full use of it according to his human nature. Now his human nature participates fully in the exercise of his majestic rule.

Jesus' ascension and his sitting at the right hand of God are also wonderful sources of comfort for Christians. Think of it. He who humbled himself to save us now rules with unlimited power and majesty over all things in heaven and on earth. He who is Lord over all is also the head of his church, his spiritual body. He uses his sovereign power for the well-being of his believers (Ephesians 1:22). He protects his church and bestows on it the gifts it needs to carry out its mission, including pastors, teachers, evangelists, missionaries, and leaders (Ephesians 4:11). He directs the affairs of this world so that all things ultimately work for the good of his believers. And he prepares a place for each individual believer in the eternal rooms of heaven (John 14:2).

He will return to judge the world

And one day that Savior will return in glory as judge of all the earth. He himself has promised to return visibly on the clouds of heaven, accompanied by his holy angels. When he returns, all the inhabitants of the earth will see him, know him, and acknowledge his lordship (Matthew 24:30,31). By the power of his almighty word, he will raise the dead, reunite their bodies and souls, and publicly pronounce judgment on all people (John 5:27-29). Believers, with bodies glorified and reunited with their souls, will be invited to share in the sinless perfection and perfect peace of eternal life with him. Unbelievers will be sent away from him forever into never-ending shame, torment, and disgrace (Matthew 25:31-46). The day of Jesus' return will be an awesome day, as the present age ends and the universe as we know it is destroyed (2 Peter 3:10). But for believers it will be a day on which they will stand up and lift up their heads, because their redemption is drawing near (Luke 21:28).

As Christ's humiliation took place for us and for our salvation, so did his exaltation. He humbled himself to be our Redeemer. His exaltation proves that his redemptive work succeeded in every way and he now rules as Lord of all. Believers can live each day in the joy and peace that flows from the assurance that their sins are all forgiven and they are reconciled with God. And they can live with the confidence that the exalted Christ will overcome all his enemies and those of the church and one day be confessed by all as King of kings and Lord of lords.

> Crown him the Lord of heav'n,
> Enthroned in worlds above;
> Crown him the King to whom is giv'n
> The wondrous name of Love.
> Crown him with many crowns
> As thrones before him fall;
> Crown him, ye kings, with many crowns
> For he is King of all. (CW 341:4)

Part III

THE THREEFOLD OFFICE OF CHRIST

9

Christ the High Priest

Jesus Christ, the wonderful person, the God-man, carried out an equally wonderful work. The work to which he was appointed and which he willingly assumed was the salvation of mankind. "The Son of Man," he himself declared, "came to seek and to save what was lost" (Luke 19:10). Whatever Jesus did and still does serves that one great purpose and is motivated by God's grace for lost mankind.

All that Jesus has done and continues to do for the salvation of the human race can be conveniently grouped under three headings, to which the church has come to refer as the "threefold office of Christ." Each of these three offices corresponds to, and can be said to have been foreshadowed by, offices instituted by God among his Old

Testament people for their benefit. Both the Old and New Testaments testify that Jesus, in response to human need, was sent to preach the gospel to the poor (Prophet). He was sent to reconcile the world to God on account of sin and to bear the punishment sinners deserve (High Priest). And he was sent to govern the church as its head and to rule the universe in the interest of his believers (King). The Old Testament prophecies present the Savior in this threefold activity. Moses speaks of a great prophet whom God would raise up, to whom all should listen (Deuteronomy 18:15-19). The psalms call the Messiah a priest (Psalm 110:4) and a King (Psalm 2:6).

Because Christ is not divided, the three offices are not divided either. Jesus did not carry out the functions of any one office independently of another. But we use the classifications suggested by the threefold office for greater clarity in presenting and understanding Jesus' work. He is our Prophet, High Priest, and King.

The name, more specifically the title *Christ* (Hebrew: "Messiah"), is used in connection with the offices of our Savior. *Christ* means "anointed one." In Old Testament times, anointing (ceremonial pouring of oil on a person's head) was a sign from God that the anointed individual was set apart by God for special service, a special task, or special work. Kings were most frequently anointed. But prophets, on occasion at least, were anointed too (Elisha: see 1 Kings 19:16). Priests were formally consecrated for the carrying out of their solemn office. In the prophecy of Isaiah 61:1, the promised Messiah speaks of himself as "anointed" with the Spirit of God. The Bible teaches that at the time of his incarnation, Jesus entered the threefold office that had been determined for him in the eternal counsels of the triune God. The Spirit's descent on him in visible form at his baptism marked his formal induction into his ministry and gave evidence that he is the unique, one of a kind, anointed one of God (Matthew 3:16).

Christ offered himself as a sacrifice for sin

As a *High Priest*, Jesus purchased grace for sinners. A priest in Scripture is one who by intercession and sacrifice aims to reconcile sinful human beings to favor with God. A priest deals with God as a mediator, on behalf of and in the place of mankind. He represents human beings before God.

In Old Testament times, God ordained an elaborate system of priests and sacrifices for his people. As the priests functioned as intermediaries between God and the people, praying and offering the prescribed sacrifices on the people's behalf, the Israelites were daily reminded of vitally important spiritual truths. They were reminded that their sins had separated them from the holy God. They were reminded that God demands payment for sins and that payment must be made on his terms alone. They were reminded that with God there can be no forgiveness apart from the shedding of blood (Hebrews 9:22). And they were reminded that the sacrifices the priests brought had atoning value only because God graciously connected them with his most significant promise. That promise, first made to Adam and Eve, then renewed to the patriarchs and to succeeding generations of God's Old Testament people, told of a Savior who would one day bring an end to this entire priestly system by offering himself as the ultimate and final sacrifice for sin. The New Testament makes it clear that the whole Old Testament priestly and sacrificial system found its ultimate fulfillment in Christ.

The work of the Old Testament priests consisted primarily in offering sacrifices on behalf of the people and interceding with God for them. The priestly office of Christ likewise consists in his work of mediation between sinners and God. He reconciled the world of sinners to God by his atoning work. And he intercedes with God continually on their behalf. The coming Savior, the Christ, was expressly called a priest in the Old Testament. Zechariah 6:13, a messianic prophecy, speaks of the Christ as "a priest on his throne." Psalm 110:4 calls the Messiah "a priest forever, in the order of Melchizedek." In the New Testament, the entire argument of Hebrews chapters 5 through 10 is that Christ is the Great High Priest who fulfilled all of the Old Testament's pictures and shadows and reconciled the world of sinners to God. The Bible's description of the priestly functions of Jesus, however, is not confined only to the passages in which the word *priest* itself is used. All references to Jesus as mediator (1 Timothy 2:5), Lamb of God (John 1:29), and intercessor (Romans 8:34) also have to do with his high priestly office and work.

As the ultimate High Priest, Jesus reconciled the sinful human race to the holy God. He did this by offering himself to God as the atoning sacrifice for the sins of all mankind. The apostle Paul in 1 Timothy 2:6 asserts that Christ "gave himself as a ransom for all men." The apostle John declares, "He is the atoning sacrifice for our sins, and not only for ours but also for the sins of the whole world" (1 John 2:2).

The unique character of Christ's priesthood is clear as we look both at his person and his work. The Old Testament priests were human. They had sins and weaknesses. The Old Testament rituals God prescribed called for those priests to first offer sacrifices for themselves and their own sins. Then they could offer sacrifices for the people they served (Hebrews 5:1-3). Jesus is the Son of God, holy and perfect. He needs no offering for himself (Hebrews 7:26,27). The Old Testament priests, of course, were distinct from their sacrifices. They offered animals on sacrificial altars, as the Mosaic Law required. And they repeated those sacrifices over and over again, day after day. Jesus served as both priest and sacrifice. He sacrificed himself on Calvary as the fulfillment of all God's promises, including the promises implied in the Old Testament priestly system. As such he became the great, ultimate, and final sacrifice for the sins of all mankind. All the previous sacrifices offered under the Old Testament system derived their value from their connection with Christ's sacrifice of himself on the cross.

Because Jesus offered himself as the ultimate sacrifice, no further sacrifices for sin will ever be needed (Hebrews 9:26). Through the high priestly work of Jesus, God is completely and for all time reconciled with sinners. And mankind is delivered from all the dreadful consequences of sin: death, the dominion of sin, and the power of the devil. The Bible constantly reminds us that our deliverance from sin through the great and perfect sacrifice of Christ is the cause and the fountain of all other spiritual and eternal blessings (Romans 8:32).

Vicarious satisfaction

Christ's work as our High Priest is sometimes described as *vicarious satisfaction*. This term, though not found in Scripture as such, has been coined by the church to describe what Scripture teaches. *Vicarious* means "substitutionary." *Vicarious satisfaction* and *vicarious atonement* are terms that have to do with the substitutionary payment that Jesus, the God-man, rendered to God in accord with

God's plan for our benefit as our High Priest and Savior. They call to mind man's sin, God's grace, and God's eternal plan to restore the sin-broken relationship between himself and sinners, thereby reconciling sinners to himself.

The justice of God demands from every human being a perfect obedience to the moral will of God (Matthew 5:48; James 2:10). It pronounces eternal condemnation as God's curse on those who fail to be perfect. Since each individual from Adam's day to our own is born a sinner and continually transgresses God's perfect law by sinful thoughts, words, and actions, every human being stands condemned as guilty before God (Romans 3:9-20). Every human being deserves God's "wrath and displeasure, temporal death, and eternal damnation."[28] The ultimate punishment God's justice demands for sin is death: physical, spiritual, and eternal death (Romans 6:23). No human being can do anything to change his or her guilty status in the sight of God. Unless God himself intervenes to rescue them, all human beings, without exception, are helpless, hopeless, and spiritually and eternally doomed.

But vicarious satisfaction, or vicarious atonement, is what God in Christ has done to rescue and save sinners who could not save themselves. As our High Priest, Jesus willingly became mankind's perfect substitute. God laid on Christ, and Christ willingly accepted in mankind's stead, the obligation both to keep the law perfectly and to bear the punishment the law demands of those who transgress it. Christ undertook that obligation, and he carried it out. He fulfilled the law perfectly in our stead. And he suffered and died to pay the penalty God's justice demanded as the ransom price for our sins and for the sins of all the world. He did it all vicariously, in our place, as our substitute, for our benefit (Isaiah 53:4-6). Through Jesus' vicarious satisfaction, his substitutionary obedience and death, God's wrath against the human race was appeased; his justice was completely satisfied.

Christ's active obedience

Christ's high priestly work was a work that involved obedience. As our substitute, he voluntarily placed himself under the Father's law and will. For want of better terms, Christ's obedience to the Father as our priestly substitute is generally described as both *active obedience* and *passive obedience*. To reconcile sinful mankind to God, our High Priest had to do two things, both requiring perfect obedience. He had to satisfy the just demands of God's holy law by keeping it perfectly (active obedience). And he had to satisfy the demands of God's justice by paying the penalty, or ransom price, that justice demanded for the sins of all the world, the penalty of death (passive obedience).

Jesus' active obedience consisted in his keeping God's law perfectly as mankind's substitute. God is holy. In the beginning he created man and woman holy and without sin. As the holy Creator, he demands, and has every right to demand, that his creatures be and remain holy, as he is holy (Leviticus 19:2). But our first parents listened to the voice of the tempter, rebelled against God, and fell into sin. Since that awful moment, all human beings are sinners. From the moment of conception, a sinful nature is passed down from parents to children. That nature hates God and is inclined only toward evil (Romans 8:7). And it reveals itself constantly in all manner of evil deeds and desires. Since the fall, no human being has been or can be perfect (Romans 3:20). No one can satisfy the just demands of God's holy law. No human being can render "active obedience" to God or earn righteousness with God by his or her actions. Without a perfect fulfillment of the law, a peaceful relationship with God is impossible. Nor can fallen human beings, by their own actions, restore that relationship, which has been broken by sin.

To satisfy God's holiness and the just demands of the law, the Son of God became man. He was born into this world without the taint of inherited sin. He was conceived by a miracle of the Holy Spirit in the womb of the virgin Mary. As mankind's substitute, Jesus placed himself under the law that God demanded human beings to fulfill perfectly. As our High Priest, he assumed all our obligations under the law. By his sinless life, he kept the law perfectly in our stead (Hebrews 4:15; 1 Peter 2:22). This was a marvelous act of humiliation. He who gave the law voluntarily placed himself under the law for us and in our place. It was a successful act of priestly substitution.

God now credits Christ's perfect keeping of the law, his active obedience, to us sinners (Romans 5:19). By virtue of our High Priest's obedience, God looks on us as having fulfilled our obligations under the law. He sees us as perfect and sinless. Thus Christ's holy life is not merely a pattern, or example, for us or some kind of prerequisite for his suffering. His active obedience is an integral part of the payment that Christ, our High Priest, offered to God for the world's redemption. The importance of Christ's active obedience cannot be overestimated or overstated. Without it, even his passive obedience would have been insufficient to complete God's plan of salvation for sinners.

Christ's passive obedience

Christ's passive obedience, on the other hand, included all that he allowed to happen to him, including and especially his suffering and death, which satisfied the demands of God's justice and paid for our sins. God is an absolutely holy and just God. He cannot and does not condone sin. He demands that every sin be punished. And he cannot and will not forgive sin unless it is paid for in accord with his demands. His justice must be perfectly satisfied. Without full atonement for sin, reconciliation between sinners and God is utterly impossible.

Since human beings cannot even begin to satisfy God's justice or offer to God a ransom sufficient to pay for any of their sins, Christ, as the ultimate High Priest, took the place of every sinner. Only he could be such a substitute, because only he is perfect God and perfect man. As mankind's perfect substitute, Jesus took upon himself every sin ever committed by every human being who has ever lived and will ever live. He took on himself the guilt of every sin. And in his perfect and awesome justice, God the Father unleashed on his sinless Son the full weight of the eternal punishment every sin deserved. It was that unfathomable burden of sin and guilt that lay on him that caused Jesus' sinless soul to be overwhelmed with sorrow. It was the eternal punishment of hell that he was bearing for every sinner that drew from his lips on Calvary that cry of anguish unlike any other ever heard: "My God, my God, why have you forsaken me?" (Matthew 27:46). His suffering of the punishment of hell for every sinner was the climax of his humiliation as well as his passive obedience.

Since by his obedience Christ fully satisfied God's justice and atoned for the sins of the whole world, God no longer charges our sins to us. Instead, he declares the debt of sin to be paid (2 Corinthians 5:19,21). By his vicarious suffering and death, Jesus satisfied the demands of God's justice. The full punishment for the sins of the world has been rendered. In Christ, God has reconciled the world of sinners to himself. Sinners are no longer liable for the punishment they deserve for their sins (Romans 5:18). Jesus has paid it all.

In Romans 5:10, Paul beautifully describes Christ's vicarious satisfaction, as it was accomplished through his obedience. "When we were God's enemies," he writes, "we were reconciled to him through the death of his Son." By his vicarious substitution Jesus took our obligations under the law and our punishment for transgressing that law. So God's wrath against sin was appeased, not by an arbitrary decree of God's power but because of the high priestly work of Christ in both his active and passive obedience. Christ's vicarious satisfaction balanced mankind's account with God. This work was done on behalf of the whole world, for every sinner, without exception (1 John 2:2). The Father showed the world that he had accepted Jesus' vicarious work by raising him from the dead (Romans 4:25). The gospel brings the good news that in Christ, God has declared peace with sinners. He has reconciled the world to himself (2 Corinthians 5:19). Through the gospel's announcement of Jesus' vicarious satisfaction, the Holy Spirit personally offers and gives to individual sinners the blessings and the new standing with God that Jesus has purchased and won for them, to be received through faith.

It was love that prompted God to reconcile the world of sinners to himself by the perfect life and innocent death of his own Son. This amazing love did not set aside his righteousness and his justice but includes it. The perfect life that God demands of us was demanded of Christ. The punishment we human beings deserved to pay for our sins was meted out to Christ.

Only Christ could have accomplished this vicarious satisfaction for us, because only Christ is the God-man. The redemption of the soul is so costly that all the treasures in the world could not have brought it about (Psalm 49:7,8). Here a rich man has absolutely no advantage over his poorest neighbor. Sinful human beings simply cannot pay the ransom God's justice demands for themselves, much less for others. Nor can a sorrow-filled heart, penitent tears, ritual sacrifices, or any amount of good deeds blot out human transgressions. The value of a sacrifice or payment for sin must measure up to the greatness of the one who needs to be appeased and reconciled. Only the sacrifice of Jesus, the God-man, could bring about the redemption of the human race. His human nature enables him to be the substitute for human beings. His divine nature gives infinite value to his sacrifice. It makes his one, great sacrifice on Calvary sufficient to atone for the sins of the whole world.

"As the High Priest," the exposition of Luther's Catechism clearly and succinctly puts it, "Christ represented the whole world before God and sacrificed himself for the sins of all."[29] If the necessity or sufficiency of Christ's high priestly work is denied, the foundation of Christian doctrine is destroyed and there is no atonement for sin. What comfort and peace fill the hearts of Christians, therefore, as the Spirit leads them to rest their faith on the rock-solid, objective foundation of the vicarious satisfaction of Jesus, our Great High Priest.

Christ intercedes for sinners

Christ's high priestly work, like that of the Old Testament priests, also included and still includes intercession for sinners with God. During his ministry on earth, Jesus frequently prayed for the spiritual welfare of those whom he had come to serve (Luke 22:32). He prayed for his disciples, and for all future believers, in his great High Priestly

Prayer recorded in John chapter 17. He prayed even for his enemies (Luke 23:34). He prayed for the wicked, that they might come to faith. He prayed for believers, that they might retain the blessings he had come to win for them and bestow on them.

In his state of exaltation, Jesus no longer needs to offer sacrifices for sins. That was accomplished once and for all by his sacrifice on Calvary (John 19:30; Hebrews 9:12). But in his state of exaltation, Christ as High Priest continues to intercede for sinners. Paul states this clearly in Romans 8:34: "Who is he that condemns? Christ Jesus, who died—more than that, who was raised to life—is at the right hand of God and is also interceding for us." On the basis of his redemptive work, finished in his state of humiliation, Jesus, now and continually in the eternal councils of God, makes intercession for sinners. The Bible pictures him as constantly reminding the Father of what he accomplished as the sinners' perfect substitute. Christ "is able to save completely those who come to God through him, because he always lives to intercede for them" (Hebrews 7:25). He constantly pleads that the merits of his atoning work be applied to sinners for their righteousness and their salvation.

Because Christ's intercession takes place within those eternal councils of the Holy Trinity, it is impossible for us to understand the exact manner in which it is carried on. But the Bible assures us that Christ's intercession for us in heaven is real. And it is effective. It is authoritative, wise, understanding, righteous, compassionate, unique, and perpetual. And it has practical value for us. When believers fall into sin, the devil, our great adversary, tries to accuse us before God. But Jesus, our high priestly advocate, constantly intercedes for us. "If anybody does sin, we have one who speaks to the Father in our defense—Jesus Christ, the Righteous One" (1 John 2:1). Christ thus renders the devil's accusations ineffectual by pointing to the fact that he has made atonement for all of our sins. It is comforting for Christians to know that our Great High Priest takes a personal interest in us and constantly pleads our cause before the Father. It is comforting to know that despite the fact that we sin daily, he shields us with the merits of his redemption, in which we place our trust.

Christ's high priestly intercession is primarily made for believers. But he also prays for the world. He prays not that the world might continue in its wicked ways but that God's time of grace for the world might be extended. He prays that more people might hear the gospel and be saved. That the world still exists and that the gospel is still proclaimed is due to the Savior's high priestly intercession. That same intercession supports believers' mission work and the gathering of souls into the Savior's kingdom. It encourages the gathering and preserving of his church.

What a comfort and source of spiritual strength it is for us Christians to know that even now in heaven, our exalted Savior is continually serving us as our Great High Priest! "He always lives to intercede for [us]" (Hebrews 7:25).

10

High Priest after the Order of Melchizedek

Jesus' high priestly office, as were his offices of Prophet and King, was foreshadowed by the priestly office as it functioned among God's people in Old Testament times. God ordained that the descendants of Aaron should serve as priests. Because they were Levites, we often refer to the Old Testament priestly order as the "Levitical priesthood." The washings and purifications, the holy garments, the refraining from wine and strong drink, all somehow foreshadowed the person and work of Christ. So did the requirements that those who served as priests were to avoid defilement and be free from physical blemish. Above all, the Old Testament priests prefigured

Christ as they offered the divinely prescribed sacrifices for sin. The entire Old Testament sacrificial system was a prophetic picture. It was a constant reminder to God's people that one day God's ultimate High Priest would offer to God the one, great, final, and complete sacrifice for sin. This Jesus did when he offered himself on the cross. The fact that God graciously connected those Old Testament sacrifices with his gospel promises and the offering for sin that Christ would render made them a kind of Old Testament means of grace. Through the sacrifices God not only assured but also actually conveyed to his people the forgiveness of sins through the coming Savior.

The New Testament epistle to the Hebrews, particularly chapters 5 through 10, provides a wonderful commentary on Christ's high priesthood and its fulfillment of everything to which the Old Testament priestly system pointed. In doing so, it shows us the similarities between the functions of the Old Testament Levitical priests and the priestly work of Jesus. It also, however, points out clear differences between the two. Hebrews 7:26 calls Jesus a High Priest who is "holy, blameless, pure, set apart from sinners, exalted above the heavens." The Levitical priests of the Old Testament were imperfect pictures of the Great High Priest. They were and remained sinners. They had to offer sacrifices for themselves, as well as for the people they served. They had to offer those sacrifices repeatedly. Jesus, the perfect High Priest, had no sin for which sacrifices were required. To accomplish his high priestly work he had to offer up only one sacrifice, the sacrifice of himself (Hebrews 7:27; 9:25,26).

The uniqueness of Christ's priesthood, as well as its superiority to the Levitical priesthood, is also demonstrated in this section of Hebrews by a reference to Christ as "a high priest forever, in the order of Melchizedek" (6:20).

Who was Melchizedek? Why was his priesthood superior to the Levitical priesthood? And why is Christ's priesthood compared to his? Melchizedek is one of the most intriguing figures in Scripture. He appears on the pages of biblical history only once, in Genesis chapter 14. There we read the story of how Abram pursued and defeated the forces of the enemy kings who had invaded Sodom and taken captive many of its citizens, including his nephew Lot. After delivering Lot and the others, Abram was met on the journey back home by Melchizedek. The Genesis text calls Melchizedek "king of Salem" and "priest of God Most High" (Genesis 14:18). Melchizedek blessed Abram. And Abram gave Melchizedek a tenth of all the spoils of war. Then, just as mysteriously as he appeared, Melchizedek disappeared. But both the writer of Psalm 110 in the Old Testament and the writer of the epistle to the Hebrews in the New describe Jesus as a "priest forever, in the order of Melchizedek" (Psalm 110:4; Hebrews 6:20). What do they mean? And what can we learn about the priesthood of Jesus from that of Melchizedek?

The name Melchizedek appears to be significant. It means "king of righteousness" (Hebrews 7:2). *Salem* is derived from the Hebrew word for peace *(Shalom)*. The religion of Noah, his son Shem, and their descendants had somehow been preserved in Salem, where Melchizedek served as both king and priest. It is evident that Melchizedek exercised a priestly function when he blessed Abram. Abram, in turn, acknowledged Melchizedek and his office by presenting Melchizedek with a tithe. Abram was a great man. God had made him great. But by his actions here, he acknowledged Melchizedek as someone worthy of his honor. If Abram acknowledged Melchizedek as greater than himself, the Bible's argument goes, Jesus' priesthood, which Psalm 110 links with that of Melchizedek, is greater than the Levitical priesthood administered by Abram's descendants from the tribe of Levi (Hebrews 7:4-9).

Psalm 110:4 refers to Melchizedek and his priesthood when it speaks of the Messiah. In this psalm we are told that David's Lord, the coming Messiah, would not only rule as a king. He would also function as a priest. His priesthood, like his kingship, would endure not only for a generation. It would endure forever. As an eternal king and priest "in the order of Melchizedek," the Messiah would exercise a priesthood superior to the Levitical priesthood. And he would offer a greater sacrifice. It is obvious that no mere mortal is described here. This unique king and priest is not only David's son. He is also David's Lord.

In keeping with the general theme of Christ's superior priesthood, the writer to the Hebrews in the New Testament notes that Jesus' priesthood fulfills God's counsels as they are revealed in the Old Testament. The Levitical priesthood and its ceremonies and ordinances are no longer in effect (Hebrews 7:18,19). Christ, the superior High Priest, has come. His priesthood is superior because it is accompanied by royal majesty. And it is eternal, as pictured by the unique appearance and priesthood of Melchizedek.

Unlike Jesus, Melchizedek was only a human being. But his mysterious appearance and disappearance in the Scriptural record picture some of the one-of-a-kind qualities of Jesus' priestly office. Nothing is said on the pages of Scripture about Melchizedek's ancestry, progeny, birth, or death. They aren't necessary to the account. He simply appears as a priest and king in this narrative. Then he disappears. The suddenness with which Scripture draws open the curtain on Melchizedek, then draws it closed again, is God's way of using this unusual figure as a picture of Jesus, whose priesthood stands apart from all others. Melchizedek appears as the only priest of his class or order. Jesus, true God and man, shares his priesthood with no other but carried out and continues to carry out the unique functions of his office by himself. The Bible speaks of no predecessor or successor to Melchizedek. Jesus' priesthood does not depend on any descent, as did the Levitical priesthood. Nor does Christ need a successor, for he abides forever in a permanent priesthood (Hebrews 7:24). And in Christ, as in Melchizedek, are combined the offices of both priest and king, something that was not permitted to the Levitical priests.

With the advent of Jesus and his unique priesthood, the Old Testament priesthood, together with the laws that governed it and the rituals that were peculiar to it, came to an end (Hebrews 8:13). They had served their purpose of foreshadowing the priesthood of Christ. Christ is the ultimate High Priest of a superior order. His sacrifice is final and avails forever. He is the only High Priest human beings need now and will ever need. He is a "priest forever, in the order of Melchizedek."

11

Christ the Prophet

A prophet, as the Bible describes the office, is an ambassador, one who speaks for God. A prophet makes known the Word and will of God to human beings. In Old Testament times, God spoke to his prophets. The prophets, in turn, reported God's message to the people. There were a number of ways in which God gave evidence to a prophet's contemporaries that the prophet had authority to speak for him. Occasionally a man's designation as a prophet was announced by the formal act of anointing. God, for example, told the prophet Elijah to anoint Elisha as his successor in the prophetic office (1 Kings 19:16). At times the office of prophet was conferred by an immediate, divine call (Jeremiah 1:7). At times the prophets were endowed with wonder-working power to establish the truth and the authority of the message they proclaimed (Exodus 4:1-9).

The message, however, was the important thing. Every Israelite was aware that there was a twofold test of a prophet's authority. First, if a prophet predicted something that did not come true, the prophet was not from God (Deuteronomy 18:21,22). True prophets spoke words that came true. Second, if a message was in accord with what God had previously revealed, the prophet was from God and his message was to be accepted. If the message was contrary to God's Word, both the message and the prophet were to be rejected (Isaiah 8:20).

Christ is the ultimate Prophet

That Christ is God's ultimate Prophet is foretold in the Old Testament and confirmed in the New Testament. In Deuteronomy chapter 18, Moses, the greatest of the Old Testament prophets, promised that God would one day raise up a prophet even greater than himself (verse 15). All people would need to listen to the words of this prophet. Isaiah too pictured the Servant of the Lord, the Messiah, as a prophet who would "preach good news to the poor" (Isaiah 61:1). Ezekiel described the Messiah as tending the flock, carrying out the prophetic function of preaching and teaching (Ezekiel 34:23). The New Testament writer to the Hebrews declared Jesus to be the ultimate Prophet when he wrote, "In the past God spoke to our forefathers through the prophets at many times and in various ways, but in these last days he has spoken to us by his Son" (1:1,2).

The people of God awaited an extraordinary prophet, whom they connected with their messianic expectations. The five thousand people Jesus fed acknowledged him as "the Prophet who is to come" (John 6:14). Hearing Jesus quote the Old Testament with an authority previously unheard, the people declared, "'Surely this man is the Prophet.' Others said, 'He is the Christ'" (John 7:40,41). Even the Samaritan woman at the well acknowledged Jesus as a prophet and associated him with the coming Messiah, who "will explain everything to us" (John 4:25). Nicodemus recognized Jesus as "a teacher who has come from God" (John 3:2). Near the end of his ministry, the Palm Sunday crowds referred to Jesus as "the prophet from Nazareth" (Matthew 21:11). After his crucifixion the Emmaus disciples called him a "prophet, powerful in word and deed" (Luke 24:19). It is true that the disciples and the people in general had a very limited and imperfect concept of Jesus' prophetic mission. Jesus himself was very clear about it. Quoting Isaiah chapter 61, he assured the crowds in the synagogue at Nazareth that this and other prophecies about the Messiah's prophetic ministry were being fulfilled in their presence (Luke 4:21). At his trial before Pilate, Jesus declared that he had come into the world to testify to the truth (John 18:37).

That Jesus is the ultimate Prophet unlike any other, the Prophet of whom all others were only shadowy pictures, is also made clear by the biblical record. Earthly prophets were anointed or called into their office when God needed them. Jesus was a Prophet from birth. At his incarnation, his human nature was endowed with the divine prophetic characteristics. From all eternity, in the councils of the triune God, Jesus was anointed as Prophet to the world (Luke 4:21). His baptism was God's public confirmation of that call and anointing. On the mountain of transfiguration, the Father not only called Jesus his Son. He commanded all to "listen to him!" (Matthew 17:5).

That Jesus is God's unique and ultimate Prophet is clear from a closer look at Deuteronomy 18:15 and its fulfillment in Christ. Moses was without question the greatest of the Old Testament prophets. No other human prophet really can be compared to him. Of all the Old Testament prophets, only Moses knew God face-to-face (Deuteronomy 34:10). But Moses foretold the coming of a prophet even greater than himself. Jesus was clearly that greater Prophet. Moses proclaimed and taught what he had received through direct communication with God. Jesus spoke his own words as the Word of God. Moses announced, "This is what the LORD says" (Exodus 7:17). Jesus could declare, "I say to all of you" (Matthew 26:64). Jesus made known the thoughts and words of God, not because he had *received* them from God but because he is God. No human being, not even the greatest teacher, can know God by himself or herself. Jesus, "the One and Only, who is at the Father's side," knows God perfectly and makes him known (John 1:18). He can do that only because he himself is God. Moses prophesied of the coming Christ. Jesus taught about himself, not as one who arrogantly usurped an authority that did not belong to him but as the eternal Word, the incarnate God.

In Old Testament times, Jesus, the second person of the Trinity, was already carrying out his prophetic work. Scripture tells us that even before his incarnation, the Son of God made known his will and his ways to Moses and the prophets by sending his Spirit into their hearts (1 Peter 1:10,11). Paul tells us in 1 Corinthians 10:4 that it was Christ who accompanied the Israelites on their wilderness journey, communicating with them through his servant Moses. The title "the angel of the LORD," as it was applied to the special, divine messenger who brought the news of the Lord's will to Hagar, Abraham, Moses, Jacob, and others was none other than the preincarnate Christ, the divine Prophet, serving as the spokesman for the Trinity.

When Jesus appeared in the flesh, he carried out his prophetic office by bringing to his contemporaries the unchanging message of divine truth. Time and again, in his teaching discussions with friends and foes, Jesus referred to the Old Testament Scriptures. "It is written" was a phrase he frequently used to direct his hearers to that which had already been revealed. Those who heard him were amazed at his knowledge and the authority with which he taught. At the same time he always made it clear that all that was written in the Old Testament Scriptures testified about him (John 5:39).

The message of Christ, the Prophet

This brings us to the truly unique feature of Christ's prophetic work. In the days of his flesh, the Son of God spoke personally and directly about himself. This made him a one-of-a-kind prophet, superior to all others who could be called prophet. Jesus and the salvation he had come to bring was the theme of his own preaching and teaching. Others had spoken of the Christ by inspiration, revealing to fellow human beings what God had made known to them. Jesus, true God and man, spoke from personal and immediate knowledge, knowledge that he possessed at all times as the eternal Word. When "the Word became flesh" (John 1:14), all the divine knowledge was communicated also to Jesus' human nature (John 21:17). With an authority possessed by no previous prophet—and no subsequent teacher—Jesus proclaims in John chapter 6 not only the good news that salvation has come but that it comes through him (verse 35). Jesus wants his listeners to understand that he came to earth to do the Father's will (verse 38). He came to carry out the plan of salvation devised in the eternal counsels of the Holy Trinity. By him and through faith in him alone, sinners are saved (verse 40). He, the incarnate Son of God, is, by his reconciling death, the life of the world (verse 51). Whoever will have life must receive it from him. In all of his preaching and teaching, in his parables and private conversations, Jesus the Prophet testified about himself. He taught with the authority of God. Many believed his testimony and were saved. That others rejected him was part of his suffering as the Great High Priest. But there could be no mistaking the fact that throughout his ministry, Jesus the Prophet revealed himself in and to the world. "For everything that I learned from my Father," he told his disciples, "I have made known to you" (John 15:15).

Jesus' primary message was the good news of the gospel. But as God's ultimate Prophet, his proclamation of God's Word also of necessity included the preaching and exposition of the law. The Sermon on the Mount, for example, is an expounding and interpreting of the law (Matthew 5–7). No, Christ was not a new lawgiver. He did not come to lay down new laws by which sinners could save themselves. When Jesus preached the law, he simply restated, explained, and applied what had already been given through Moses. He used the law in the service of the gospel, to expose the sins of those to whom he was eager to proclaim the good news of God's forgiving love in him through the gospel. Jesus also used the law to guide those who through the gospel had been brought to faith in him as they strove to live their new lives as his people. Jesus' chief prophetic function, however, was to preach the gospel. This he did, beautifully, continually, and clearly, as he made himself known to those to whom God had sent him as the fulfillment of all of God's promises to Israel and to the nations.

Christ continues to serve as the Prophet

Jesus' prophetic work, like his high priestly work, did not cease after his ascension into heaven. He continues to function as Prophet "mediately," that is, through his believers, his church. The apostles received the gospel as a sacred trust to carry to the ends of the earth. As the preincarnate Christ inspired the authors of the Old Testament Scriptures through his Spirit, the ascended Christ, through that same Spirit, inspired the evangelists and apostles to commit his teachings to writing in the books of the New Testament (John 16:13; 1 Corinthians 2:13). With the inspired Scriptures as an infallible guide, Christ has now entrusted his prophetic office to his believers of every age. Believers are called to testify of the Savior and declare his praise until he returns again in glory (1 Peter 2:9). All the teaching that is taking place in the church now, all the teaching that will continue to take place until Jesus comes again, as it is based on the sacred Scriptures, continues and extends the prophetic office of the ascended Savior.

To those who carry out his commission to "make disciples of all nations" (Matthew 28:19), Jesus promises his abiding presence and his unfailing blessing. Yes, to his church on earth, Jesus gives pastors, teachers, and evangelists as special gifts (Ephesians 4:11). But it is not only through their witness but through the faithful, joyful testimony of every believer that Jesus' prophetic work continues among us today and will continue until the end of time. In accordance with God's design, Jesus did his teaching and preaching primarily among the Jews (Matthew 15:24). After his resurrection and ascension, it is God's will that the good news of Jesus and his salvation be carried to every nation, tribe, language, and people, to the ends of the earth (Acts 1:8). God grant that also through our personal witness and our joint efforts to take the good news of Jesus everywhere, Christ's prophetic office and work may indeed continue, as he wills it, until he comes again.

12

Christ the King

At the heart of the hopes of God's Old Testament people lay the promise of a king. Psalm 110:1, "The LORD says to my Lord: 'Sit at my right hand until I make your enemies a footstool for your feet,'" was a well-known prophecy emphasizing the kingly functions of the Messiah. So was the promise through Jeremiah: "I will raise up to David a righteous Branch, a King who will reign wisely" (23:5). To David himself was given the promise that from his descendants would arise a king unlike any other, a king who would establish and rule over an everlasting kingdom (2 Samuel 7:13). The people of Jesus' day also associated the titles and functions of a king with the coming Messiah. Unfortunately, they did this almost to the complete exclusion of his prophetic and priestly functions. This was because their idea of the Messiah as king had been twisted and reshaped according to their own human wants and desires. They were looking for a king who would bring them material prosperity and peace, not spiritual blessings. Conflict with the occupying Romans only heightened the hope for a political conqueror-king. Those who expected an earthly king, however, were disappointed in Jesus. Following the feeding of the five thousand, some wanted to make him king (John 6:15). But by the end of that same chapter, we find that after Jesus revealed the intensely spiritual nature of his mission and his kingdom, many turned away from him in resentment and disappointment (verse 66).

But Jesus was, and is, the King. Even in his state of humiliation, he was the King unlike any other. Even in his humiliation, he was ruler of the universe. "All that belongs to the Father is mine," he told his disciples in the upper room (John 16:15). In his well-known conversation with Pilate, Jesus acknowledged that he is a king (John 18:37). But he also made it clear that he is not an earthly king (verse 36). He had not come to earth to be a rival to Herod or to Caesar. The Bible's teaching concerning Jesus' kingdom is both instructive and encouraging to his believers. He is our King. And we are his loyal subjects.

A king has power and authority to rule. That the Savior of mankind is the King is frequently and distinctly asserted in Scripture, both directly and by implication. Jesus' kingdom, however, is not a place. It has no physical boundaries nor the trappings of an earthly kingdom as we think of them. Rather, Jesus' kingdom is an activity. It consists of his ruling activity and the exercise of his kingly prerogatives. As true God, Jesus is King over all things and from all eternity. By virtue of his incarnation, his royal rule was bestowed also on his human nature. During his life on earth, even in his humiliation, Jesus displayed his kingship in various ways. His miracles, for example, revealed his kingly rule over sickness and disease, even over death. In the depth of his suffering, he remained the eternal King, promising a place in his kingdom to the penitent thief dying at his side (Luke 23:43). In his exaltation, Jesus has taken up the full use of his ruling authority according to his human nature. He sits at God's right hand as King and ruler of all things. And he will return again in glory at the end of time as King and judge.

In defining Jesus' kingly functions, it has become customary to speak of his ruling activity as threefold. Jesus rules in the *kingdom of power*, the *kingdom of grace*, and the *kingdom of glory*. These distinctions are human ways of trying to describe divine activity. They can't perfectly tell the story of Jesus' kingly rule. And there are areas that overlap. But this threefold description of Jesus' rule is certainly a helpful guide to our understanding of what the Bible means when it refers to Jesus as the King.

Christ's kingdom of power

When we speak of Jesus' rule in his kingdom of power, we refer to his rule over the entire universe. The kingdom of Jesus is not limited in any way. It extends over all creatures, visible and invisible, as well as the whole universe. Jesus himself declares that all authority in heaven and on earth belongs to him (Matthew 28:18). The Father has placed all things under his feet, also according to his human nature (Ephesians 1:22). There is nothing over which Jesus doesn't rule. As King in the kingdom of power, Jesus upholds all things by his powerful word. He controls the forces of nature and the destiny of nations. Without his will not even a sparrow falls to the ground. Good and evil, even the demons and the damned, are subject to him. He is King of kings and Lord of lords. Ephesians 1:20-23 emphatically describes Christ's rule of the universe: "God placed all things under his feet and appointed him to be head over everything" (verse 22).

Christ's kingdom of grace

The kingdom of grace is Christ's gracious activity of gathering and preserving his believers, his church. By means of the gospel, he brings people to saving faith and blesses the church with all manner of spiritual gifts. By his power he effectively guards the church against all its enemies. The members of the kingdom of grace are not all human beings but only those who, by the Spirit's gracious work in their hearts through the gospel, have been brought to believe on Jesus as Savior and Lord. Jesus himself describes this kingdom as a kingdom established not by war and bloodshed, not by civil laws, but by God's Word (Matthew 28:19,20).

The kingdom of grace is invisible to the naked eye. It exists in human hearts (Luke 17:20,21). Nevertheless, this kingdom is stronger than all the earthly kingdoms that have existed and will exist. The world's great empires all have their day in the sun, then pass away. The ancient Greek and Roman empires are history. The influence of the British and French empires has ceased. The Soviet Union has toppled. Jesus' kingdom of grace outlasts them all. It continues in spite of persecution, ridicule, and falsehood. And it will exist in human hearts wherever the gospel is proclaimed until the end of time (Matthew 16:18).

Jesus established this kingdom by defeating his and mankind's spiritual enemies as he carried out his atoning work. It is called the kingdom of grace because it is Jesus' promise and offer of grace that wins sinners for the kingdom and the reception of grace by Spirit-wrought faith that makes them members of this kingdom. Appreciation of grace moves those who belong to the kingdom of grace to render willing obedience and service to the King. It was Jesus' kingdom of grace that was prophesied in the Old Testament, Daniel chapter 2, as a rock that broke all other kingdoms into pieces and grew to fill the whole earth (verses 35,44). Jesus' well-known kingdom parables in Matthew chapter 13 describe the growth, the infinite value, and the lasting nature of his kingdom of grace.

The essence of Jesus' kingdom of grace, then, is nothing external. It is the saving rule of Jesus in the hearts of his believers. For individuals the kingdom consists in a personal relationship with Christ established through the Holy Spirit's work in their hearts. This kingdom comes when Christ comes into human hearts and lives. Luther described that spiritual process in his explanation to the Second Petition of the Lord's Prayer: "God's kingdom comes when our heavenly Father gives his Holy Spirit, so that by his grace we believe his holy Word and lead a godly life now on earth and forever in heaven."[30]

Where the Word of the gospel is proclaimed to sinners, Christ exercises his saving rule, his kingdom of grace. Only God, of course, can see into human hearts. Only he knows who the individual members of this invisible kingdom are (2 Timothy 2:19). But we know that the kingdom of grace is present wherever the gospel is preached and the sacraments are used. These are the means by which the Holy Spirit works to create and strengthen faith in human hearts. To all who are led by the Spirit to acknowledge him as Savior and Lord, Jesus gives gifts for service in his kingdom (1 Corinthians 12:4-11). And through the gospel, the Holy Spirit preserves believers against the attacks of the spiritual enemies and keeps them safe as members of his kingdom of grace (2 Timothy 4:18).

Christ's kingdom of glory

In the kingdom of grace, Jesus rules over his *church militant*, the church of believers struggling with their enemies and the enemies of their faith here on earth. In the kingdom of glory, he rules over the *church triumphant*. The kingdom of glory exists not on earth but in heaven, where Christ has all glory. Those who are faithful unto death receive eternal crowns of glory and honor (Revelation 2:10). Everlasting joy and unrestricted communion with Christ, together with the Father and the Holy Spirit, are the happy lot of the members of the kingdom of glory. The souls of believers enter the kingdom of glory at the moment of their physical deaths (Philippians 1:23). Following the resurrection, their bodies too will share in the joy and perfection of the kingdom of glory (1 Corinthians 15:42-44).

As there are no unbelievers or hypocrites in the kingdom of grace, so there will be no unbelievers in the kingdom of glory. Only the elect will enter that kingdom. The elect are those who have been chosen in grace by God from all eternity (Ephesians 1:4-6). They have been brought into his kingdom of grace and preserved as faithful members of that kingdom by the gospel. In the kingdom of glory, they will participate with all the holy angels in the joys of heaven. They will see God face-to-face (1 Corinthians 13:12).

In the consummate kingdom of glory, the triune God—Father, Son, and Holy Spirit—will rule. Each person of the Trinity will participate in that rule, including the Son, whose kingdom is an everlasting kingdom. In the kingdom of glory, Christ will finally deliver the struggling church on earth from all its enemies and from the evils that trouble it, and he will translate it into the church triumphant. In Luke 22:29,30 Jesus promises his disciples, "I confer on you a kingdom, just as my Father conferred one on me, so that you may eat and drink at my table in my kingdom and sit on thrones, judging the twelve tribes of Israel." That promise was not just for the 11 believers gathered with the Savior that night. It was for all believers of every age and place, including each of us.

"My kingdom is not of this world" (John 18:36) also holds true for the kingdom of glory. This kingdom will not find its realization here on earth, as many falsely teach. The Bible does not promise that paradise will be restored here on earth. Nor does it teach that Christ will return for a glorious thousand-year reign here on earth. The kingdom of glory will exist only in the world to come. That makes its existence a matter of faith for us. We look forward to it longingly, as pilgrims in this earthly valley of tears. As we journey through life in this sinful world, we Christians are cheered and encouraged by Jesus' promise of heavenly glory. And we know that the way to those heavenly rooms, which are even now being prepared for us, is only through him (John 14:2-6).

Our poor human imaginations are not even able to visualize anything that can be compared with the blessedness in store for us in the church triumphant in heaven (1 Corinthians 2:9). The gifts that Jesus our King will bestow on us in the kingdom of glory will be unlike anything we have ever experienced here on earth. In that kingdom we will be forever free from sin, temptation, trouble, tears, sickness, suffering, pain, and death (Revelation 21:4). As we by faith await our entrance into the kingdom of glory, an entrance which will take place either at the time of our physical deaths or when Jesus returns, we will be moved by thankful appreciation and eager expectation of its promised blessings. We will gladly live, work, and even suffer for our King during our lives on earth. And when at last we enter the kingdom of glory, we will thank and praise him in sinless perfection and perfect joy forever.

The relationship among the three kingdoms

While we distinguish three phases of Christ's kingdom, or rule, we can't separate them, as if they had nothing in common. There is a close relationship among all three. One King rules. And there is one dominant purpose in his rule. Christ rules in his kingdom of power for the benefit of his kingdom of grace (Ephesians 1:22). Christ, the supreme ruler of the universe, is at the same time the head of the church, his body. That means he exercises his lordship and power over all things in the interest of his spiritual body, his believers. At times he restrains the actions of the wicked so that the church is not harmed. At other times he uses even the wicked actions of the church's enemies to serve his own purposes, notwithstanding their evil intentions. Jesus governs the world in his rule of power so that he might gather and build his church (kingdom of grace) by bringing sinners to faith and preserving them in faith. He encourages believers to carry out his Great Commission by assuring them that "all authority in heaven and on earth has been given to me" (Matthew 28:18) and

"Surely I am with you always, to the very end of the age" (Matthew 28:20).

What a comfort it is to know that the one who commissioned us to share the gospel in all the world is the sovereign Ruler of the universe! What an encouragement it is to know that he promises to go with us as we carry out that awesome task! He who rules in the kingdom of power assures us that the salvation of sinners is not merely a side issue as he governs the world. It is the chief issue. He rules in his kingdom of power for the benefit and upbuilding and preservation of his kingdom of grace.

Likewise, Christ's rule in his kingdom of grace ultimately serves the kingdom of glory. Christ's purpose in building his church in the world through the gospel is not to build a visible organization or serve temporal interests. But the chief purpose of Christ's rule in his kingdom of grace is to win and prepare souls for his kingdom of glory.

As long as they are in the world, Christians are the salt of the earth (Matthew 5:13). By their influence they can and should counteract and testify against the moral corruption of the world around them. And Christians are the light of the world, holding out the light of the gospel to those without the truth in a sin-darkened world (Matthew 5:14). As Christians continue to be salt and light in the world, God extends the world's time of grace. And each day that passes provides more opportunities for the gospel to be proclaimed and for the kingdom of grace to come to individual human hearts.

But the ultimate purpose of the kingdom of grace is achieved when sinners are safely brought into the kingdom of glory. Believers' hope in Christ is not for this world only. But Christians are born again into a living hope that does not fade or disappear, Peter tells us in his first epistle

(1:3,4). There is an inheritance reserved in heaven for us. One day we will receive the fullness of that inheritance. In the kingdom of glory, the knowledge that is imperfect now, as we possess it through the gospel, will be complete and perfect. We will see God and know him perfectly and forever (1 Corinthians 13:12). So Christ's rule in his kingdom of power benefits his kingdom of grace. And the kingdom of grace finds its ultimate completion in the kingdom of glory.

The doctrine of the kingly office of Christ is a doctrine that calls for faith. We can't see with our physical eyes or comprehend with our mental powers that Christ rules over all things. Sometimes, Luther wrote, it appears as if not Christ but the devil is on the throne. For that reason the Bible teaches about Christ's kingdom of power very carefully and goes into great detail about what it means. The means of grace are perceptible, but the kingdom of grace is invisible. It exists in the hearts of believers. Only through faith in the promises of Scripture are we assured that "the kingdom of God is within [us]" (Luke 17:21) and that in spite of all the opposition of the devil, false teachers, and the world, the church will abide forever. Nor do we know or have we experienced what the kingdom of glory will be like. But by faith we look forward to sharing in it. We rejoice in the hope of the glory of God. Under the protection of him who rules in his kingdom of power we live each day as thankful, energetic members of his kingdom of grace. And our gaze is directed, and rightly so, to the kingdom of glory as we live in hope. Under his rule in the kingdom of power and the kingdom of grace, we now await the kingdom of glory with a bold and joyful confession: "Jesus is my King."

Part IV

THE WORK OF CHRIST

13

Redemption

The work of Christ is *redemption*. *Redeem* means to "buy back" or "set free by means of the payment of a ransom." The fact that Christ's work is called redemption reminds us that though salvation is free, it is not cheap. Nor was it cheaply won. The holy God, who hates sin and demands that every sin be punished, doesn't simply forgive sins by executive order. To do that would be to ignore, or at the very least to compromise, his own holiness. But God declares sinners righteous in his sight because he has received and accepted a ransom payment for human sin, a payment that fully and completely satisfied the demands of his justice and holiness. That Jesus paid the ransom by his vicarious atonement has already been discussed in connection with our study of Christ's high priestly work. We review that same work here from a slightly different perspective as we consider the words of Martin Luther's explanation to the Second Article of the Apostles' Creed: "He has redeemed me."[31]

Jesus paid the ransom

To reconcile sinful human beings to a holy God, a ransom had to be paid that was sufficient and acceptable to him. No earthly sacrifices, no blood of bulls and goats could provide cleansing for sin (Hebrews 10:4). No human riches, including all the world's silver and gold, were sufficient to pay the ransom. No human being could offer him- or herself as a ransom for any other human being. Psalm 49:7-9 tells us, "No man can redeem the life of another or give to God a ransom for him—the ransom for a life is costly, no payment is ever enough—that he should live on forever and not see decay." Heartfelt sorrow and penitent tears are not a sufficient ransom for sin either. Nor can a lifetime of good works make amends for a single sin.

Sometimes, to us at least, the sins we commit seem small. But their guilt must be measured against the sinless perfection of the one against whom they are committed, God himself. And the value of the ransom must measure up to the greatness and holiness of the one who is to be appeased and conciliated. No man or beast or riches, but God alone can satisfy his own divine justice and reconcile a world of guilty sinners to himself.

If Christ had not been true God, his life and death could not have been a sufficient ransom for our sins. But Christ is God. That makes his ransom sufficient and our redemption complete. The value of Christ's ransom lies not in the amount of blood he shed—something that medieval theologians foolishly debated—nor in the duration and intensity of his suffering, although that was prescribed by God. The divinity of Jesus' person, the fact that he was and is truly God, is the absolute guarantee that his sacrifice is acceptable to God and that in his blood and death God provided a ransom sufficient to satisfy himself. "For you know that it was not with perishable things such as silver or gold that you were redeemed from the empty way of life handed down to you from your forefathers, but with the precious blood of Christ, a lamb without blemish or defect. He was chosen before the creation of the world, but was revealed in these last times for your sake" (1 Peter 1:18-20).

To reconcile us to God by paying the ransom that God's law required and his justice demanded, Jesus had to do two things. He had to satisfy the demands of God's holiness by keeping the law perfectly (active obedience). And he had to satisfy the demands of God's justice by accepting the punishment that justice demanded for the sins of all mankind (passive obedience).

God is holy. He made our first parents holy and now demands, as the perfect Creator, that all human beings be holy. To meet his demands, it is necessary to keep his law perfectly. Since the fall no human being can do this. And without a perfect fulfillment of the law, reconciliation with God is impossible. To satisfy the demands of the law, therefore, and to make good for our shortcomings, the Son of God became man. He placed himself under the law as our substitute that he might keep the law and fulfill it in our stead. During his life Jesus kept the law perfectly and fully, not for himself, because he is above the law, but for us who are under the law. His holy life, his satisfaction of the demands of God's holiness through a perfect keeping of the law, is essential to his redemptive work for us.

Just as essential was Jesus' passive obedience, his innocent suffering and death as our substitute. Again, since no human being can pay a suitable ransom, Jesus took the world's place. The Father charged to him, and he willingly accepted, all the sins of the whole world. In the suffering of Christ, God declared his justice, which demands punishment for the sins of all. By his blood and death, Jesus atoned for all the sins of the whole world. His resurrection proves that his ransom payment was sufficient. As a result, God no longer charges our sins to us but forgives them. The ransom payment was made to God. And because Jesus is God, together with the Father and the Holy Spirit, it can rightly be said that he who rendered the satisfaction and he who received it are one and the same.

Jesus' redemption was universal. He did not pay a ransom only for believers, although it is only believers who receive the benefits of redemption. The Bible is very explicit in stating that Christ took away the sins "of the world" (John 1:29). There is objective comfort for all sinners in the knowledge that Jesus' redemptive work is universal. The word *world* is a word into which each of us can write his or her own name. And as we do that, we can be sure beyond all doubt that when the Bible says that Jesus redeemed the world by the payment of ransom, the ransom was paid for each of us, without exception, for each of us as individuals.

In answer to the question, Why did Christ have to redeem you? our catechism exposition answers, "By nature we are slaves of sin, death, and the devil."[32] Jesus' redemption broke the stranglehold that our spiritual enemies had on our souls and on our lives. It set us free from the power and dominion of those enemies, free to live for and serve the Savior, who emancipated us by his redemptive work as our perfect substitute.

Redemption from sin

Jesus redeemed us from sin. Sin has been in the very fabric of our being from the moment we were conceived. Sin has infected the whole human race from the moment our first parents fell into sin. We all inherit a sinful nature from our parents.

Sin brought with it God's condemnation. Sin angers God. Eternal condemnation is the punishment that sins deserve. The apostle Paul in Romans uses the expression "slaves to sin" in describing all human beings as they are by nature (Romans 6:17). A slave is someone who has no power of his own but is under the control of someone else and has to do that other person's bidding.

As our Redeemer, Jesus set us free from sin. Jesus, of course, did not become our substitute by committing sin for us. The fact that we are sinners cannot be undone. To understand what it means that Jesus redeemed us from sin, we need to distinguish between sin and the guilt of sin. Because we are sinners by what we are (inherited, or original, sin) and by what we do (actual sin), the guilt of sin rests on us from the moment we are conceived. But in his work of redemption, all our guilt was charged to Christ. He assumed all the blame, all the responsibility for our transgressions. Though we are and remain sinners, the guilt of the sins of the whole human race was charged to him. The sinless one, he who "had no sin," willingly and voluntarily was made "to be sin for us" (2 Corinthians 5:21). All the guilt of our sins was charged to him. His perfect righteousness and payment for sin by his death are credited to us. Now we, though sinners, stand righteous before the judgment seat of God (Romans 8:1).

As Jesus bore our guilt, so he also took our punishment. He redeemed us "by becoming a curse for us" (Galatians 3:13). He suffered the eternal death we deserved for sin. He died the accursed death we should have died. Now the good news of forgiveness, the gospel of redemption, declares us free from the curse and the guilt of our sins. Declared free from our sins, their guilt and punishment, and moved by the Spirit to personally receive by faith what Jesus earned for us, we are freed from the accusations of our consciences and motivated to live godly lives. We look forward without fear to standing before the judgment seat of God. We ourselves are still sinners. We live in a sinful world. And the general consequences of sin remain: the struggles, the trouble, the disease and pain, the physical death. But in Christ we are forgiven sinners. We have been given new spiritual life through the gospel. As God's redeemed children, we have his promise that the general consequences of sin we experience in this world are not punishments but loving, fatherly chastening intended for our good (Hebrews 12:7-11).

Christ's redemptive work has also set us free from the ruling power of sin in our lives. In our natural spiritual state, we can do nothing but sin. But by virtue of Jesus' redemption, believers in Christ are free from the power and control of sin in their personal lives (Romans 6:14). Believers are still plagued by the old Adam, the sinful nature, which never gives up trying to reassert its control of our lives. But in Christ believers also have a new nature, or new man, that is able to resist and fight against sin. That new nature is now the dominant force in believers' lives. And we who follow Christ, encouraged and empowered by the Holy Spirit as he works in our hearts through Word and sacraments, daily battle against sin and strive to live our new lives for our Savior (Galatians 5:24,25).

Redemption from death

Christ has redeemed us from death. God did not originally create human beings to die but to live with him forever in perfect communion. Sin, however, corrupted the human race and brought death into the world in its wake. Because our lives are infested with sin, we deserve death (Romans 6:23). We deserve not just physical death but eternal death, eternal separation from God in hell. Death is separation. Spiritual death is the separation of the soul from God. Temporal (physical) death is the separation of the soul from the body. Eternal death is the complete and unending separation of both body and soul from God in the fiery depths of hell. Spiritual death, the separation of the soul from God, is the condition in which every human being enters the world. It is the spiritual condition all inherit from the time our first parents fell into sin. Our natural inclinations in this state of spiritual death lead us not toward God but away from him. Nor do we possess the will or the power to change that condition. Had Christ not redeemed us from death, we could have never had a relationship with God. We would not have been able to believe in God, to love or fear him. We would have remained in the darkness and despair of spiritual death as we lived out our lives here on earth. And at physical death we could have looked forward only to eternal separation from God in hell.

But by suffering death on the cross, a death in which he suffered hell in our place, Christ redeemed us from death. He set us free from the curse and the power of death

(Hebrews 2:14). The Holy Spirit's work in human hearts through the gospel rescues individual sinners from spiritual death. As the Spirit touches hearts with the gospel's living power through Baptism or the Scriptures, he makes those who by nature are spiritually dead spiritually alive (Colossians 2:13). He creates in human hearts that faith which takes hold of Jesus and his redemptive blessings and restores the sin-broken relationship between sinful human beings and the holy God. All who by faith take hold of Jesus and his spiritual blessings have, by Jesus' own definition, "crossed over from death to life" (John 5:24). They possess spiritual and eternal life.

Even though believers in Christ are, by faith in Jesus, spiritually alive, they still experience physical death. As long as this world stands, death will always be "the last enemy" (1 Corinthians 15:26), the last and greatest of all the consequences of sin in a sinful world. And because we human beings weren't originally created to die, we will always have a natural fear of death.

The fact that Jesus has redeemed us from death, however, completely changes the meaning of physical death for believers. And it comforts us and fills us with hope as we deal with death or as we face it ourselves. Because Jesus has redeemed us from death, physical death is not a punishment for believers. Nor does it lead to an eternal separation from God. It is merely a change of existence. At the very moment believers' souls separate from their bodies in physical death, they are with the Lord in eternal life (John 11:25,26). And when Jesus returns on the Last Day, he will raise all the dead and reunite their bodies and their souls. The bodies of believers will be glorified like Jesus' own glorious body, and believers, both body and soul, will be with Jesus in the glory of the resurrection life (Philippians 3:21).

That is why believers need not "grieve like the rest of men, who have no hope" (1 Thessalonians 4:13), when believing loved ones are taken from us by physical death. That is why each believer can look confidently forward to his or her physical death with the attitude expressed by the apostle Paul, "I desire to depart and be with Christ, which is better by far" (Philippians 1:23). And that is why believers can confess together with sure conviction, "I believe in . . . the resurrection of the body and the life everlasting." Jesus has redeemed us from death.

Redemption from the power of the devil

Finally, Jesus has redeemed us from the power of the devil. By leading Adam and Eve into sin, the devil gained power over all mankind. Now, as they are born into the world, all people are not members of God's family but of Satan's. "He who does what is sinful," the Bible says, "is of the devil" (1 John 3:8). The devil continually seeks to exercise his control over each individual by leading him or her ever deeper into sin. As he does that, he makes use of powerful allies: the sinful world and each human being's own sinful nature. By ourselves, we are utterly helpless against the devil and his temptations. And whenever we sin, the Bible pictures the devil as accusing us before God, demanding that we too share in his eternal fate. We cannot deny the charges. By nature we are helpless slaves of the devil. We belong to him and are dominated by him.

But the Bible also tells us that the Son of Man, Jesus, appeared on earth "to destroy the devil's work" (1 John 3:8). Jesus defeated the devil when as our substitute, he successfully resisted the devil's temptations and when by his innocent suffering and death, he fully paid the ransom price God's justice demanded for our sins and our guilt. By his redemptive work as our substitute, Jesus purchased and won deliverance from the power of the devil for all people. And those who by the Spirit are brought to faith in Jesus enjoy freedom from Satan, from his temptations and accusations, and from his dominating power in their lives. In the strength of faith, believers can resist temptation (James 4:7). Yes, because of the weakness of the sinful flesh, believers still fall into sin. But even when they sin, the devil cannot accuse them before God (Revelation 12:10,11). Jesus acts as their advocate, their lawyer, before the Father's bar of divine justice (1 John 2:1). Satan doesn't stop his relentless attacks. He continues to tempt us when and where we are most vulnerable, and he will continue to do so as long as we live. But by God's grace and by the power of the Holy Spirit working in us through the gospel, we are enabled to resist the devil. We win more and more victories over temptation. And we live our lives no longer as Satan's slaves but as God's children and his willing servants in Christ.

The purpose of Christ's redemption

The purpose of Christ's redemptive work is summarized by Martin Luther in his words of explanation to the Second Article: "All this he did that I should be his own, and live under him in his kingdom, and serve him in everlasting righteousness, innocence, and blessedness, just as he has risen from death and lives and rules eternally."[33]

Our Savior's redemptive work may be said to have both a *long-term* and a *short-term* purpose. The long-term purpose is an eternal one. By virtue of Jesus' redemptive work, the holy God has declared the world of sinners righteous in his sight. Believers personally receive the blessings Jesus has won for them by faith (individual justification). At the same time, believers receive from the Spirit a new life, a life that really is life, spiritual and eternal life. This life consists in a peaceful, blessed relationship with God and the continual assurance of God's forgiving love during a believer's life here on earth. And it includes a life of sinless perfection in the glory of the world to come. The believer's new life in Christ does not consist in just the few years we spend here on earth. But it is an endless, eternal life. This life passes safely through death and the grave to timeless eternity. The long-term purpose of Christ's redemptive work, therefore, is that sinners might enter and enjoy forever the ultimate gift of the eternal life that God bestows on his believers in the world to come.

But God doesn't generally call human beings into his spiritual kingdom of grace and then take them immediately into his eternal kingdom of glory. How are believers, then, to regard the time "in between," the time that they as Christians spend in this sinful and imperfect world? It is in this connection that we can speak about the short-term, or immediate, purpose of our Savior's redemption. Simply stated, the short-term purpose of Jesus' redemption is that believers use the time God has given them here on earth to live for him and to serve him with the new lives the Holy Spirit has given them. We call believers' lives lived for the Savior here on earth lives of *sanctification*. Lives of sanctification are lives lived by believers as people set apart for God, for his special purpose.

The apostle Paul calls attention to this short-term purpose of Jesus' redemption in Ephesians 2:10. The preceding verses, Ephesians 2:8,9 constitute the "great grace passage" of the New Testament: "It is by grace you have been saved, through faith . . ." Then the apostle immediately follows the great salvation passage with the words of verse 10: "For we are God's workmanship, created in Christ Jesus to do good works, which God prepared in advance for us to do." Combine these two passages and you discover the great truths about the purpose of our redemption. Christ has redeemed us not only *from* sin, death, and the power of the devil but also *for* an express purpose: "That I should be his own, . . . and serve him," as Luther says in the Small Catechism. Christ has redeemed us not only for eternal life with him (long-term purpose) but also for immediate service to him in lives of good works here on earth (short-term purpose).

The Christian's life of love and thankful service to the Lord is the subject of another book in this series. But it is certainly appropriate to refer to it here. When the Bible urges us to serve the Lord, it is not speaking of a slavish kind of service that results from fear of punishment but the kind of willing, loving service that flows from thankful faith. The very same love of Christ that sets us free from sin, death, and the devil makes us eager to serve him and our fellowmen, as it shines into our hearts and transforms our lives (Romans 12:1,2). God himself provides the guidelines for such service in his Word, specifically in the Ten Commandments. Daily we ask for the good judgment and sanctified common sense that will enable us to apply the principles and truths expressed in the commandments in a loving way to the various situations we face in life. As God's redeemed children, we will serve him continually in "righteousness, innocence, and blessedness" here on earth. We will serve him faithfully on earth until he takes us to be with him in the eternal glory that we know will be ours, because "he has risen from death and lives and rules eternally."

Endnotes

¹*This We Believe: A Statement of Belief of the Wisconsin Evangelical Lutheran Synod* (Milwaukee: Northwestern Publishing House, 1999), p. 11.

²*Christian Worship: A Lutheran Hymnal* (Milwaukee: Northwestern Publishing House, 1993), p. 18.

³Martin Luther, *Luther's Works*, St. Louis (German) Edition, Vol. 7, page 1263ff., as quoted by Francis Pieper in *Christian Dogmatics*, Vol. 2 (St. Louis: Concordia Publishing House, 1951), p. 64.

⁴*Christian Worship*, p. 18.

⁵Carl E. Braaten and Robert W. Jensen, *Christian Dogmatics*, Vol. 1 (Philadelphia: Fortress Press, 1984), p. 527, as quoted by Wilbert Gawrisch in *Who Is Jesus Christ?* (Milwaukee, Northwestern Publishing House, 2002), p. 30.

⁶*Christian Worship*, p. 133.

⁷John Schaller, *Biblical Christology* (Milwaukee: Northwestern Publishing House, 1981), p. 49.

⁸Johann Conrad Dietrich, *Kleiner Katechismus* (St. Louis: Concordia Publishing House, 1904), question 34, as quoted by Pieper in *Christian Dogmatics*, Vol. 2, p. 70.

⁹Martin Luther, *Luther's Works*, American Edition, Vol. 34, p. 210, as quoted by Wilbert Gawrisch in "The Twentieth Century

Crucifixion of Christ," *Our Great Heritage*, Vol. 2, edited by Lyle W. Lange (Milwaukee: Northwestern Publishing House, 1991), p. 487.

[10] Paul Tillich, *Systematic Theology*, Vol. 2 (Chicago: University of Chicago Press, 1957), p. 94, as quoted by Wilbert Gawrisch in *Who Is Jesus Christ?* p. 45.

[11] Gawrisch, "The Twentieth Century Crucifixion of Christ," p. 502.

[12] Gawrisch, "The Twentieth Century Crucifixion of Christ," pp. 485,486,496,503.

[13] Hans Schwarz, *What Christians Believe* (Philadelphia: Fortress Press, 1987), p. 40, as quoted by Patsy A. Leppien and J. Kincaid Smith in *What's Going On among the Lutherans?* (Milwaukee: Northwestern Publishing House, 1992), p. 80.

[14] Wilfred S. Bunge, *Theological Perspectives* (Decorah, IA: The Department of Religion, Luther College, 1962), p. 52, as quoted by Gawrisch in "The Twentieth Century Crucifixion of Christ," p. 503.

[15] *Christian Worship*, p. 133.

[16] *Luther's Catechism* (Milwaukee: Northwestern Publishing House, 1998), p. 5.

[17] Martin Chemnitz, *The Two Natures in Christ*, translated by J. A. O. Preus (St. Louis: Concordia Publishing House, 1971), p. 64.

[18] Formula of Concord, Solid Declaration, Article VIII:66, *The Book of Concord: The Confessions of the Evangelical Lutheran Church*, translated and edited by Theodore G. Tappert (Philadelphia: Fortress Press, 1959), p. 604.

[19] Johannes Quenstedt, as quoted by John Theodore Mueller in *Christian Dogmatics* (St. Louis: Concordia Publishing House, 1953), p. 270.

[20] Quoted by Mueller in *Christian Dogmatics*, p. 265.

[21] The rest of this paragraph draws from the material by Mueller in *Christian Dogmatics*, pp. 265-267.

[22] Paul O. Wendland, "Now That God Is One of Us: A Study of the Communication of Attributes in the Person of Christ," in *We*

Believe in Jesus Christ, edited by Curtis A. Jahn (Milwaukee: Northwestern Publishing House, 1999), pp. 88-90.

[23] *Christian Worship,* p. 133.

[24] Martin Luther, *Luther's Works,* edited by Jaroslav Pelikan and Helmut F. Lehmann, American Edition, Vol. 22, (St. Louis: Concordia Publishing House; Philadelphia: Fortress Press, 1955–1986), p. 110.

[25] Martin Luther, *What Luther Says,* Vol. 1, p. 195, as quoted by Wilbert Gawrisch in "The Practical Application of the Two Natures of Christ," *Our Great Heritage,* Vol. 2, p. 463.

[26] Formula of Concord, Solid Declaration, Article VIII:65, p. 604.

[27] This interpretation of 1 Peter 3:18 is given by Siegbert Becker in "The Christological Flesh-Spirit Antithesis," *Our Great Heritage,* Vol. 2, pp. 554-570.

[28] *Luther's Catechism,* p. 320.

[29] *Luther's Catechism,* p. 158.

[30] *Luther's Catechism,* p. 7.

[31] *Luther's Catechism,* p. 5.

[32] *Luther's Catechism,* p. 161.

[33] *Luther's Catechism,* p. 5.

For Further Reading

The Book of Concord: The Confessions of the Evangelical Lutheran Church, translated and edited by Theodore G. Tappert. Philadelphia: Fortress Press, 1959.

    The Augsburg Confession, Article III, The Son of God

    The Small Catechism, Creed, The Second Article

    The Large Catechism, Creed, The Second Article

    Formula of Concord, Epitome/Solid Declaration: Article VIII, Person of Christ

    Formula of Concord, Epitome/Solid Declaration: Article IX, Christ's Descent into Hell

Gawrisch, Wilbert R., *Who Is Jesus Christ?* Milwaukee: Northwestern Publishing House, 2002.

Jahn, Curtis A., Editor. *We Believe in Jesus Christ: Essays on Christology*. Milwaukee: Northwestern Publishing House, 1999.

Lange, Lyle W., Editor. "Section Four: Jesus Christ Is the Mediator of Salvation." Essays in *Our Great Heritage*, Volume 2, pp. 418-625. Milwaukee: Northwestern Publishing House, 1991.

Schaller, John. *Biblical Christology*. Milwaukee: Northwestern Publishing House, 1981.

Scripture Index

Genesis
    3:15—18
    14:18—115

Exodus
    3:14—17
    4:1-9—120
    7:17—122

Leviticus
    19:2—105

Deuteronomy
    18:15—120,122
    18:15-19—100
    18:21,22—120
    34:10—122

2 Samuel
    7:13—127

1 Kings
    19:16—100,119

Psalms
    2:6—100
    2:7—15
    16:9,10—81
    49:7,8—109
    49:7-9—140
    51:5—29
    110—15,116
    110:1—127
    110:4—100,102,115,116

Isaiah
    8:20—120
    9:6—15
    53—71
    53:3—28
    53:4-6—104
    53:9—81

61—121
61:1—100,120

Jeremiah
1:7—119
23:5—26,127

Ezekiel
34:23—120

Daniel
2:35,44—131

Zechariah
6:13—102

Matthew
1—26
1:18—37
1:20—37
1:23—13,37
3:16—101
3:17—17
4:1-11—78
5–7—124
5:13—135
5:14—135
5:48—104
7:28,29—17
8:27—57
9:2—17
12:6—17
12:8—17
12:22-29—17
12:39—90
13—131
15:24—126
16:13—7
16:13-17—44
16:15—7
16:16—7,15
16:18—15,130
16:21—89
17:5—18,121
21:11—121
22:21—79
24:30,31—95
24:36—78
25:31-46—96
26:12—26
26:18—75
26:30—27
26:38—27
26:42—27
26:48,49—65
26:64—122
26:65-67—27
27:26—27
27:35—27
27:46—27,80,107
27:57-60—81
28:12-15—87,88
28:18—57,129,134
28:18-20—16
28:19—125
28:19,20—130
28:20—16,58,94,135

Mark
6:2,3—79
6:3—27

Luke
1:32,33—44

1:35—13,15,37
1:42—26
1:47—29
2:11—60
2:21—78
2:52—78
3—26
4:21—121
9:28-36—59
17:20,21—130
17:21—136
19:10—99
21:28—96
22:29,30—133
22:32—109
22:51—75
23:34—110
23:43—129
24:19—121
24:39—26
24:41-43—91
24:44—89
24:50,51—93

John

1—21
1:1,2—13,36
1:3—15
1:14—44,59,123
1:18—122
1:29—102,142
1:51—27
2:19—92
2:24,25—57
3:2—121
3:6—29
3:34—57
4:6—65
4:25—121
5:17,19—75
5:19,20—17
5:23—17,57
5:24—146
5:27-29—95
5:39—123
6—37
6:14—121
6:15—128
6:35—17,123
6:38—124
6:40—124
6:51—124
6:66—128
7:40,41—121
8:40—26
8:58—54
10:14—17
10:17,18—80
10:18—89
10:30—16,38,75
10:33—17
10:38—38
11:25,26—146
11:33-35—65
11:35—27
13:5—79
14:2—95
14:2-6—133
15:15—124
16:13—125
16:15—128
17—110
18:4-6—75
18:36—128,133

18:37—121,128
19:30—110
19:35—88
21:17—123

Acts
1:3—93
1:8—93,126
1:9—93
2:24—92
2:25-31—89
2:29-36—88
2:31—81
3:15—54
13:37—81

Romans
1:4—90
3:9-20—104
3:20—105
4:25—90,108
5—26
5:10—108
5:18—108
5:19—106
6:14—144
6:17—143
6:23—104,145
8:1—144
8:7—105
8:32—103
8:34—102,110
9:5—16,26,44
12:1,2—150

1 Corinthians
2:8—54
2:9—133
2:13—125
10:4—122
12:4-11—132
13:12—132,136
15:12-14—88
15:17—90
15:20—91
15:26—146
15:42-44—132

2 Corinthians
5:19—108
5:19,21—107
5:21—91,143
8:9—75

Galatians
3:13—144
3:16-19—26
4:4—13,18,37
5:24,25—145

Ephesians
1:4-6—132
1:20,21—94
1:20-22—84
1:20-23—130
1:22—95,129,130,134
2:8,9—149
2:10—149,150
4:10—57
4:11—95,125

Philippians
1:23—132,147
2:6-11—71,76,77

2:7—72,75
2:8—64,77,79
2:9—84
2:9-11—57
3:21—92,146

Colossians
1:16—15
1:20—64
2:9—45,57,58,59,76
2:13—146
2:15—85

1 Thessalonians
4:13—147

1 Timothy
2:5—26,102
2:5,6—39
2:6—102
3:16—15,42,49

2 Timothy
2:19—131
4:18—132

Hebrews
1:1,2—120
1:2—15
2:11—65
2:14—146
2:17—65
2:18—65
4:15—66,79,106
4:16—31
5–10—102,114
5:1-3—103

6:20—115
7:2—115
7:4-9—116
7:18,19—116
7:24—117
7:25—110,111
7:26—29,30,114
7:26,27—103
7:27—114
8:13—117
9:12—110
9:22—101
9:25,26—114
9:26—103
9:27—85
10:4—140
12:7-11—144
13:8—16,54

James
2:10—104
4:7—148

1 Peter
1:3,4—136
1:10,11—122
1:18-20—141
1:19—29
2:9—125
2:22—106
3:18—153
3:18,19—85
3:18-20—85

2 Peter
3:10—96

1 John
- 1:7—66
- 2:1—111,148
- 2:2—102,108
- 3:8—60,147
- 5:6—59
- 5:20—16

Revelation
- 2:10—132
- 12:10,11—148
- 17:14—95
- 21:4—134

Subject Index

active obedience 105,106
actual sin 143
adoptionist monarchians 20
anointing 119
apotelesmatic genus 60-62
apotelesms 60,61
applications of doctrine of Christ's two natures 63-67
Arianism 21,22
ascension 92-94
Athanasian Creed 26

baptism of Christ 17
"beggar's cloak" 71-81,84
Bible and Christ as true God 14-18
Bible and Christ as true man 26-28
brother 65,66
Bultmann, Rudolf, 33,87

Chemnitz, Martin, 41
Christ and creation 15
Christ as sacrifice for sin 101-103
Christ as true God 13-24
Christ as true man 25-34
Christ remained true God during humiliation 73-76
Christ, title, 100
Christian Science 20,23
communication of idioms 51-62
communication of natures 45,46
communion 52,53
communion of natures 45,46
communion of properties 51-62
conception and birth 77,78
Council of Chalcedon 22,46,47

Council of Constantinople 22
Council of Nicaea 22

death, redemption from, 145-147
Definition of Chalcedon 45
descendant of patriarchs 26
descent into hell 84-86
divine call 119
Docetism 31-33

Ebionites 19,20
eternal death 145
Eutyches 47
Evangelical Lutheran Church in America (ELCA) 34
exaltation of Christ 71-96

false teachings against Christ as true God 18-24
false teachings against Christ as true man 31-34
false teachings against the personal union 46-49
Father-Son relationship 15,16
Formula of Concord 43,44

genera 53
Gnosticism 32,33
great exchange 90,91

hallucination theory 87
High Priest 30
High Priest, office of, 99-117
history of Christ's humiliation 77-81

human nature of Christ described 28-31
humiliation of Christ 71-96
hypostatic union 42

idiomatic genus 53-56
idioms 52
immediate call 119
inherited sin 143
intercession 109-111

Jehovah's Witnesses 22
"Jesus Seminar" 22,23,55,56
judge of the world 95,96

kenoticism 75,76
King, office of, 127-136
kingdom of glory 132-136
kingdom of grace 130-132,134-136
kingdom of power 129,130,134-136

majestic genus 56-60
mediately 125
Melchizedek 113-117
message of Christ 123-125
modal monarchians 20
monarchianism 20,21
Mormons 22

necessity for our salvation 65
Nestorius 46,47,55
New Age Movement 23

original sin 143

Subject Index

passive obedience 105-109
Paul of Samosata 21,55,59
person of Christ 13-67
personal union 41-49
personality of Christ 30
"phantom man" 26,32,33
physical appearance of Christ 30
physical death 145
pious fraud 87
power of the devil, redemption from, 147,148
properties 52
Prophet, office of, 119-126
public ministry 78,79
purpose of redemption 148-150

ransom paid 140-143
real presence 47
redemption 139-150
relationship of the two natures 42-45
resurrection 86-92
return to power and glory 83-96

Samosatenes 21
sanctification 149

Schweitzer, Albert, 33
scientology 23
sin, redemption from, 143-145
sitting at the right hand of God 94,95
Socinians 21,23
state of exaltation 72
state of humiliation 72
subordinationist 19
suffering, death, and burial 79-81

temporal death 145
threefold office 99-136
Tillich, Paul, 33
transfiguration 18,59

Unification Church 23
unitarian 19
unitarianism 23
universal redemption 142

vicarious atonement 103-105
vicarious satisfaction 103-105
virgin birth 35-39

work of Christ 139-150

Zwingli, Ulrich, 47,55,58,59